A REPORT OF THE
CSIS PROLIFERATION
PREVENTION PROGRAM

Nuclear Trade Controls

MINDING THE GAPS

January 2013

Author
Fred McGoldrick

50 YEARS | CHARTING OUR FUTURE

CSIS | CENTER FOR STRATEGIC & INTERNATIONAL STUDIES

About CSIS—50th Anniversary Year

For 50 years, the Center for Strategic and International Studies (CSIS) has developed solutions to the world's greatest policy challenges. As we celebrate this milestone, CSIS scholars are developing strategic insights and bipartisan policy solutions to help decisionmakers chart a course toward a better world.

CSIS is a nonprofit organization headquartered in Washington, D.C. The Center's 220 full-time staff and large network of affiliated scholars conduct research and analysis and develop policy initiatives that look into the future and anticipate change.

Founded at the height of the Cold War by David M. Abshire and Admiral Arleigh Burke, CSIS was dedicated to finding ways to sustain American prominence and prosperity as a force for good in the world. Since 1962, CSIS has become one of the world's preeminent international institutions focused on defense and security; regional stability; and transnational challenges ranging from energy and climate to global health and economic integration.

Former U.S. senator Sam Nunn has chaired the CSIS Board of Trustees since 1999. Former deputy secretary of defense John J. Hamre became the Center's president and chief executive officer in April 2000.

CSIS does not take specific policy positions; accordingly, all views expressed herein should be understood to be solely those of the author(s).

Cover photo: Taken from Fairport Harbor of the nuclear power plants in the distance in Perry, Ohio. Credit: Scott Smithson, 2010. www.flickr.com/photos/dtwpuck/sets/72157622671484328/

ISBN 978-0-89206-762-6

Center for Strategic and International Studies
1800 K Street, NW, Washington, DC 20006
Tel: (202) 887-0200
Fax: (202) 775-3199
Web: www.csis.org

CONTENTS

ACKNOWLEDGMENTS

The author would like to acknowledge Sharon Squassoni, director of the Proliferation Prevention Program, for commissioning this report and providing many helpful comments on the text, and Leah Fae Cochran for her help putting the final product together. This report was made possible by the generous support of the John D. and Catherine T. MacArthur Foundation.

EXECUTIVE SUMMARY

The merits of nuclear trade controls for helping stem proliferation have been strenuously debated for decades. Some have maintained that the policy of secrecy and denial that the United States pursued in the aftermath of Hiroshima and Nagasaki was a failure and that, instead, sharing the peaceful benefits of nuclear energy under nonproliferation controls and conditions has helped build key elements of the global regime to prevent the spread of nuclear weapons. Others argue that international nuclear trade increases the risk of nuclear-weapons proliferation. The first view highlights a country's motives for acquiring nuclear weapons such as national security concerns, domestic politics, or national prestige and emphasizes providing security assurances and building norms, rules, and institutions to discourage the spread of these weapons. The second view stresses technological capabilities and the likelihood that the diffusion of nuclear technology makes proliferation more likely. This view targets denying countries know-how and equipment. Both viewpoints have merit, and both need to be taken seriously.

Most of the nine countries that possess nuclear weapons today acquired their nuclear arsenals primarily through dedicated military programs, clandestine and illegal procurements, and deliberate assistance from nuclear-weapon states and not through the diversion of imported civil nuclear materials and equipment subject to nonproliferation controls. Most civil nuclear programs are peaceful in nature, and the vast majority of states with such programs are abiding by their nonproliferation commitments. Suppliers have employed their nuclear trade policies as a means of establishing the widely accepted principle that states wishing to take advantage of the peaceful applications of nuclear energy must make effective commitments not to misuse that technology for nuclear explosive purposes and to accept adequate verification of those obligations.

Nevertheless, international peaceful nuclear commerce and assistance carry with them real risks of diversion to nuclear weapons. Among other things, reactor-grade plutonium produced in nuclear power plants is usable in nuclear weapons; enrichment and reprocessing facilities can produce weapons-usable nuclear materials that are vulnerable to diversion by both states and subnational actors to build nuclear explosives; and reprocessing plants are difficult and expensive to safeguard. In addition, states can try—and have tried—to use peaceful nuclear cooperation as a means of acquiring skills for developing nuclear weapons. Nuclear-weapon aspirants have also justified imports for their peaceful nuclear programs as a cover for developing a nuclear-weapons capability. Some nuclear suppliers, particularly in the early decades of the nuclear era, exported sensitive technology with little consideration of its security consequences or provided nuclear assistance without adequate controls and assurances.

Wherever one stands on the relative risks and benefits of civil nuclear trade, nuclear power and civil nuclear trade are unlikely to disappear. In fact, several recent reports have projected their continued growth and expansion to additional countries. One of the key challenges facing the United States and other major nuclear suppliers is to ensure that this projected growth in commercial nuclear power, if actually realized, will not lead to the proliferation of nuclear weapons. Strengthening nonproliferation controls and conditions on peaceful nuclear trade are indispensable to meeting this challenge.

This report has four main elements. First, it explains the nature and importance of the nonproliferation conditions that the United States requires for its exports of nuclear materials, equipment, and technology as well as dual-use items and technology that have both nuclear and nonnuclear applications. Second, it compares these with the nuclear export controls of other exporting states as reflected in the guidelines of such multilateral arrangements as the Zangger Committee (ZC), the Nuclear Suppliers Group (NSG), and other international agreements and understandings such as the Treaty on the Non-Proliferation of Nuclear Weapons (NPT) and, where known, the specific export policies of other individual nuclear-supplier states. Third, it assesses the limits, weaknesses, successes, and failures of nuclear export controls of nuclear suppliers to date. Finally, it identifies the challenges for the future and the role that the United States should play in meeting them.

Nonproliferation Controls on Peaceful Nuclear Cooperation

The United States and other major nuclear suppliers generally require non-nuclear-weapon states to give assurances and guarantees as a condition of nuclear cooperation. Over time, suppliers have learned lessons—sometimes painfully—that they need to insist on unambiguous and comprehensive nonproliferation assurances, close loopholes, exercise special restraint and caution in exporting sensitive materials and technologies, control even some nonnuclear items and technology, and demand robust and comprehensive inspections as a condition of nuclear supply.

PEACEFUL, NONEXPLOSIVE USE ASSURANCES. An essential condition for civil nuclear trade is an assurance by recipient states of peaceful, nonexplosive use. It is also fairly uncontroversial, because 184 non-nuclear-weapon states (plus Taiwan) that have ratified the NPT have already undertaken this commitment. The U.S. Atomic Energy Act (AEA), as amended by the Nuclear Non-Proliferation Act of 1978 (NNPA), bans the use of any peaceful nuclear export by the United States for "any nuclear explosive device, or for research on or development of any nuclear explosive device, or for any other military purpose." The prohibition on military uses of exports is not found in the NPT, the ZC, or the NSG guidelines, but the statute of the International Atomic Energy Agency (IAEA) bans the use of agency assistance from furthering any military purpose. The U.S. ban on nuclear explosive use is more specific and comprehensive than the prohibitions found in the NPT ("the manufacture or acquisition" of nuclear explosives), the ZC (the "diversion to nuclear weapons or other nuclear explosives"), or the NSG ("uses which would result in any nuclear explosive device"). However, the differences in these formulations do not appear to have had any practical implications to date.

SAFEGUARDS. Another essential requirement for international nuclear commerce is the application of safeguards to all nuclear material in a non-nuclear-weapon state, known as comprehensive or full-scope safeguards. (The NPT requires non-nuclear-weapon states to accept such safeguards on all their peaceful nuclear activities.) But other safeguards requirements are also critically important, including the extension of safeguards beyond the term of a peaceful nuclear cooperation agreement or a treaty (known as perpetuity of safeguards); the expansion of the authority of the IAEA in applying safeguards as set forth in the Additional Protocol to IAEA safeguards agreements; a back-up system for IAEA safeguards, or "fall-back" safeguards; and safeguards in nuclear-weapon states (which are not required by the NPT, are voluntary in nature, and cover only their civil nuclear facilities).

Comprehensive Safeguards. The NPT does not obligate suppliers to impose comprehensive safeguards as a condition of nuclear supply. Rather, the treaty requires suppliers to place safeguards only on their exports of nuclear materials and nuclear equipment to nonparties to the treaty. A few suppliers, including the United States and Canada, adopted comprehensive safeguards as condition of supply in the late 1970s, but most nuclear exporters imposed only the NPT requirement until the early 1990s, thus allowing states such as Argentina, Brazil, and India to obtain nuclear supplies while resisting safeguards on all their nuclear activities.

The NSG adoption in 1993 of comprehensive safeguards as a condition of nuclear supply to non-nuclear-weapon states harmonized supplier policies and made the requirement for comprehensive safeguards on exports a general international norm. However, that norm has been seriously undercut by the actions of China, Russia, and the United States. The new NSG guideline required comprehensive safeguards only on new nuclear commitments—the so-called grandfather clause. It also allowed a safety exception, which permitted nuclear exports without the comprehensive safeguards requirement when they were deemed essential for the safe operation of existing safeguarded facilities. Both Russia and China cited one or the other or both as justification for their nuclear cooperation with India and Pakistan. In addition, the United States concluded an agreement with India that did not require comprehensive safeguards and persuaded the NSG to carve out an exception for India from its comprehensive safeguards guideline.

Perpetuity of Safeguards. Perpetuity of safeguards on nuclear materials ensures that safeguards continue to apply to nuclear materials even if an agreement expires, is terminated, or is suspended. U.S. law requires that safeguards continue to apply to items subject to a U.S. agreement even if that agreement terminates or expires or if the cooperating partner withdraws from the NPT. The NSG guidelines call for perpetuity of safeguards, but they do not apply to supply contracts concluded before April 3, 1992. The principle of perpetuity of safeguards is now widely accepted international practice among suppliers. However, the NPT contains a significant loophole. If a non-nuclear-weapon state validly withdraws from the NPT, its safeguards agreement would no longer be in force. Nevertheless, parties to most nuclear-weapon-zone treaties and members of the European Atomic Energy Community (EURATOM) made safeguards commitments that would endure regardless of their NPT membership.

Additional Protocol. The Additional Protocol (AP) expands the IAEA's authority and practices to gain increased information about, and access to, a state's nuclear activities and greatly enhances its ability to detect illegal, clandestine activities. The United States has included the AP in some recent agreements. With the entry into force of the AP in the U.S. voluntary safeguards agreement with the IAEA in 2009, the United States is now in a more credible position to insist on the AP in new agreements. Neither the NSG nor the 2010 NPT Review Conference has been able to agree on requiring the AP as a condition of supply for nuclear items or to declare the AP "the IAEA safeguards standard." The Non-Aligned Movement insists on the voluntary nature of the AP, a stance that is unlikely to change in the next three years under Iran's chairmanship of the group. Nevertheless, as of October 2012, 119 states plus EURATOM and Taiwan have an AP in force. The AP is gaining acceptance as an international norm, but some important holdouts such as Argentina, Brazil, and Egypt remain.

Fall-Back Safeguards. If the IAEA is not applying or cannot apply safeguards in a country or if a state withdraws from the NPT and renounces its NPT safeguards agreement, fall-back safeguards give the supplier government the right to insist that some other form of safeguards be applied to the nuclear materials covered by its agreement. U.S. policy requires fall-back safeguards provisions in post-NNPA agreements for peaceful nuclear cooperation. The NSG has also adopted a guideline on fall-back safeguards, but it does not apply to agreements or contracts before April 3, 1992. To date, no state has implemented any kind of fall-back safeguards, but they remain an important instrument in ensuring the perpetuity of verification if the IAEA cannot apply safeguards or if a state renounces its NPT safeguards agreement.

Safeguards in Nuclear-Weapon States. Safeguards on nuclear exports to nuclear-weapon states are not required by U.S. law, the NPT, the ZC, or the NSG. The United States requires some form of verification in its agreements with nuclear-weapon states, and all the NPT nuclear-weapon states have entered into voluntary safeguards agreements with the IAEA that designate facilities as eligible for IAEA safeguards but allow for the withdrawal of such facilities from safeguards.

PHYSICAL PROTECTION. U.S. agreements typically require the application of the criteria set out in the Convention on the Physical Protection of Nuclear Material (CPPNM) and the NSG guidelines (which are identical). More recent agreements require the implementation of the IAEA recommendations contained in INFCIRC/225. The CPPNM prescribes only very general levels of physical protection and leaves much to the discretion of each government in applying specific measures. INFCIRC/225 sets out far more detailed measures for the security of nuclear materials and facilities. While the NSG guidelines take note of the IAEA recommendations, they do not require them as a condition of supply. Physical protection is universally regarded as the sovereign responsibility of a state, and many countries strongly resist a standardized set of measures or any international review of their security systems.

TRANSFERS OF SENSITIVE NUCLEAR TECHNOLOGY. Suppliers exercise special restraint in the transfer of enrichment and reprocessing because such technologies can produce materials that can be directly used in a nuclear weapon. Virtually all U.S. agreements for peaceful nuclear cooperation prohibit the transfer of these sensitive nuclear technologies under those agreements. As a matter of policy, the United States does not export sensitive nuclear technology. U.S. laws also provide for the cutoff of economic and military assistance or nuclear exports to countries that transfer or receive enrichment or reprocessing technology.

The original NSG guidelines called for the exercise of restraint in the export of sensitive nuclear technology. In June 2011, the NSG adopted a revised guideline that, among other things, limits the transfer of enrichment and reprocessing only to a state that is in compliance with its nonproliferation objectives, is an NPT party, and meets agreed standards of safeguards, physical protection, and safety. U.S. and NSG policies on such exports go beyond the requirement of the NPT, which does not control technology transfers. Most other major nuclear-supplier states have not followed the United States in adopting a declared policy refraining from transfers of sensitive nuclear technology. However, the few transfers of enrichment and reprocessing technology and equipment by major nuclear suppliers have been made to states that already possess such capabilities, and most recent transfers involved enrichment technology to the United States. (Clandestine and illicit transfers of such technologies by non-NSG members—Pakistan and North Korea—have threatened to undermine the nonproliferation regime.) Requiring special controls on transfers of enrichment and reprocessing technology and equipment has become standard practice among major nuclear suppliers but has been the subject of heated debate within the NSG, the IAEA Board of Governors, and the NPT Review Conference. Many non-nuclear-weapon states insist that they have rights under the NPT to possess such facilities.

EXPORTS OF WEAPONS-USABLE MATERIALS. The United States does not export plutonium for peaceful purposes and has had a long-standing objective of eliminating civil uses of highly enriched uranium (HEU). In addition, U.S. law imposes special restrictions on HEU exports. The NSG imposes no explicit ban on exports of plutonium or HEU for civilian purposes but calls for restraint in the export of weapons-usable materials. The Declaration of Common Policy of the European Union places requirements on the transfer of plutonium and HEU among member states. The "Guidelines on the Management of Plutonium" (INFCIRC/549) adopted by the major plutonium holders also contain conditions on the transfer and retransfer of plutonium.

PRIOR CONSENT RIGHTS. U.S. agreements for peaceful nuclear cooperation contain a guarantee by the cooperating country that it will not enrich, reprocess, or otherwise alter in form or content U.S.-obligated nuclear material; store weapons-usable material; or retransfer any U.S.-obligated nuclear materials or equipment without the prior approval of the United States.

The United States gives consent in some agreements to enrich up to 20 percent U-235, while other agreements require consent for any enrichment. The NSG guidelines have no provision for consent to the enrichment of supplied materials, but some suppliers require consent for all enrichment or enrichment above 20 percent. The United States has exercised its consent rights on reprocessing in different ways depending on the political and security relationship it has with its cooperating partners, the status of their civil nuclear programs, their nonproliferation credentials, and the proliferation concerns in the regions in which they are located. For example, during the 1970s, the United States granted consent on a shipment-by-shipment basis to certain states to transfer their spent fuel into EURATOM for reprocessing while retaining approval rights on the further disposition of the recovered plutonium. In 1977, the United States gave limited approval to Japan to reprocess a specified amount of spent fuel at its Tokai-Mura reprocessing plant for two years.

The U.S. agreements with Norway and the United Arab Emirates (UAE) grant advance consent on a one-time basis to transfer U.S.-obligated spent fuel from these countries to EURATOM for reprocessing but retain consent rights over any subsequent disposition of the recovered plutonium and uranium. The United States grants so-called programmatic consent to reprocessing and the subsequent disposition of recovered plutonium in its agreements with Japan and EURATOM, i.e., consent covering the entire civil nuclear program of these states. U.S. agreements with Japan and Switzerland provide consent to transfer U.S.-obligated spent fuel to EURATOM for reprocessing and the return of the recovered plutonium and uranium for use in the Japanese and Swiss civil nuclear programs. The United States has also given advance consent to the reprocessing of U.S.-obligated spent fuel in safeguarded Indian reprocessing facilities (yet to be constructed) and the use of the recovered plutonium and uranium in safeguarded Indian reactors. The United States has retained a right to suspend its consent in these agreements if required by nonproliferation or national security concerns.

The United States has also imposed special restrictions in regions of political instability and proliferation concern. The U.S.-Egypt agreement for peaceful nuclear cooperation requires any reprocessing of U.S.-obligated nuclear material and any storage or fabrication of plutonium recovered as a result of such reprocessing to take place in facilities outside Egypt. The U.S.-UAE agreement for peaceful nuclear cooperation bans the UAE from possessing enrichment and reprocessing facilities.

The consents described above are not the norm. For most of its cooperating partners, the United States discourages reprocessing and plutonium use, and most U.S. cooperating partners have neither requested nor been granted prior U.S. consent to the reprocessing or alteration in form or content of spent fuel. In a few cases, the United States has rebuffed informal requests for reprocessing.

The NSG guidelines call for consent rights "whenever appropriate and practicable," leaving it to the individual supplier how to interpret such a phrase. Policies and practices are not uniform among suppliers. Both Australia and Canada routinely include these consent rights in their bilateral agreements and gave programmatic consent to reprocessing to EURATOM and Japan. Russia has been taking back spent fuel from its customers. France and the United Kingdom provide reprocessing services to other states but require their customers to take back the recovered plutonium, uranium, and nuclear waste. However, plutonium returns have been made only to Japan and to states in Western Europe such as Germany and Switzerland. Australia, Canada, and the United States have actually granted consent to the reprocessing of spent fuel to only a few countries—France and the United Kingdom (in the U.S.-EURATOM agreement), Japan, and India. France has given consent to India to reprocess.

RETROACTIVITY AND PERPETUITY OF NONPROLIFERATION CONDITIONS. Post-NNPA, U.S. agreements for peaceful nuclear cooperation apply retroactively to the previous agreements that they replaced; for example, nuclear material and equipment that had been subject to a pre-NNPA agreement become subject to the full panoply of assurances and controls of the new post-NNPA agreement. Nuclear material that was free of certain U.S. consent rights under an old agreement becomes subject retroactively to those consent rights under the post-NNPA agreement. It is not known whether other nuclear suppliers have adopted a similar requirement. In addition, all the nonproliferation conditions and controls in U.S. agreements for peaceful nuclear cooperation will continue in effect even if a peaceful nuclear cooperation agreement terminates, expires, or is suspended. The NSG guidelines provide for the perpetuity of safeguards but not for the other nonproliferation guarantees and assurances contained in the guidelines.

DUAL-USE AND CATCH-ALL EXPORT CONTROLS. The United States has long controlled the exports of dual-use items and technology—that is, those that have both nuclear and nonnuclear uses. It has also had "catch-all" controls to prevent the export of any items that are not on an export control list if intended for nuclear explosive devices or unsafeguarded activities. The NSG did not adopt dual-use controls until 1992 and a catch-all control mechanism until 2004.

TERMINATION OF NUCLEAR COOPERATION AND RIGHT OF RETURN. U.S. law specifies a number of actions by a non-nuclear-weapon state that would require the suspension of U.S. nuclear exports but allows the president to waive such suspension if he determines that it would be seriously prejudicial to the achievement of U.S. nonproliferation objectives or would otherwise jeopardize the common defense and security. The NSG calls for consultations if one or more members believe that a recipient has violated a supply agreement or IAEA safeguards or engages in nuclear explosive activities. The NSG guidelines provide for suspension of nuclear items to states that violate their nonproliferation obligations but allow for a "safety" exception if safeguards are applied to the relevant facilities. U.S. law contains no such explicit exception. In addition, the grounds for terminating U.S. nuclear cooperation are far more extensive than those contained in the NSG guidelines. Cases of actual termination or suspension of nuclear exports have been few in number.

U.S. agreements for peaceful nuclear cooperation contain a right to require the return of U.S.-obligated nuclear material and equipment, if the cooperating partner violates certain nonproliferation norms. The NSG also provides for a right of return, but this guideline does not apply to agreements or contracts drawn up on or before April 3, 1992, and its grounds for exercising a right of return are less extensive than those of the United States. No supplier has ever exercised a right of return. Such a right is largely symbolic, since suppliers would likely face formidable legal, political, and practical hurdles to taking back spent nuclear fuel or other irradiated materials or equipment.

Agenda for the Future

Some supplier states have in the past acted irresponsibly by placing commercial or strategic considerations above nonproliferation interests. A few continue to do so today. Russia and China have exploited the so-called grandfather and safety clauses of the NSG guidelines to supply nuclear reactors and fuel to India and Pakistan. The United States concluded a peaceful nuclear cooperation agreement with India without insisting on comprehensive safeguards and then persuaded the NSG to approve an exemption from its comprehensive safeguards requirement for India. The selective interpretation of NSG guidelines or the exemption of a recipient state from them does not bode well for the effectiveness of the export control regimes of the major nuclear suppliers. These actions can only lead to charges of hypocrisy and undermine the NSG's legitimacy in the eyes of nonmembers.

The absence of dual-use and catch-all control systems by most major suppliers until the early 1990s also made it possible for several nuclear-weapon aspirants to acquire numerous items for their nuclear-weapons programs.

Policies for controlling nuclear exports cannot solve or even address all proliferation challenges. Even the most effective nuclear export policies of the NSG cannot prevent nonmembers such as Pakistan or North Korea from deliberately undermining the effectiveness of international nuclear export controls and of the nonproliferation regime itself. Such behavior has to be addressed through other means such as vigorous diplomatic pressure, sanctions, interdiction measures like the Proliferation Security Initiative, or, in the extreme, preemptive military action.

Despite their limitations and gaps, the nuclear export policies of the major nuclear suppliers have had some success in increasing the costs and risks of the procurement efforts of such states as Pakistan, Iran, and Iraq and in delaying their acquisition of sensitive nuclear facilities or nuclear weapons. Moreover, if the major suppliers had not forged an agreement on common rules of the game, supplier states would have been tempted to improve their competitive position in the international market by minimizing the nonproliferation conditions on their nuclear exports.

The export policies of the United States and other major suppliers must remain an essential component of the nonproliferation regime for a number of reasons:

- They provide an essential complement to the NPT without violating the rights of the parties to the treaty. The NPT is the indispensable, albeit imperfect, foundation of the international nonproliferation regime. By requiring comprehensive and fall-back safeguards, physical protection, rules for technology transfers, controls on dual-use items, and sanctions for violations of nonproliferation norms, nuclear export controls of suppliers have bolstered the effectiveness of the nonproliferation regime in essential ways that the NPT by itself does not cover.
- They serve as legal and normative barriers to the misuse of civil nuclear programs for nuclear explosive or military uses.
- They provide a basis for terminating nuclear cooperation and the imposition of international sanctions if a recipient violates nonproliferation norms and commitments.
- They increase the costs and risks of the procurement efforts of nuclear-weapon aspirants and delay the acquisition of sensitive nuclear facilities or nuclear weapons.
- They uphold the basic principles of the nonproliferation regime, namely, (1) that states should be eligible to reap the benefits of the peaceful uses of nuclear energy only if they make effective commitments against nuclear explosive or military purposes and accept adequate verification of those commitments and (2) that international peaceful nuclear cooperation cannot take place unless the public and national governments have confidence that it is firmly based on nonproliferation assurances designed to prevent the diversion of civil nuclear programs to explosive purposes.

Nuclear export controls have evolved over time to keep pace with technical innovations and political developments and in response to various challenges to the nonproliferation regime. The major suppliers are much better positioned today than in the past to block the international procurement efforts of aspiring nuclear-weapon states and to prevent the diversion of global nuclear commerce to nuclear explosive uses.

Still more needs to be done. Supplier states have a special responsibility for and interest in supporting an effective international nuclear nonproliferation regime. Such a regime is necessary to assure the public and national governments that international commerce in civil nuclear energy is being effectively controlled and that proliferation risks associated with the atom are manageable. In the absence of such confidence, governments will not license nuclear exports and imports, the public will oppose the development of nuclear power, and the nuclear industry will not accept the risk of investment in nuclear technology.

The major nuclear suppliers need to adopt new and strengthened export controls to keep pace with the emerging nonproliferation challenges ahead:

ENSURING THE INTEGRITY AND COMMONALITY OF EXPORT CONTROLS. In general, the United States has a more stringent and more encompassing set of nonproliferation conditions than other suppliers. In the past, this disparity had a significant impact particularly when many other suppliers did not require comprehensive safeguards or dual-use export controls. It is hard to measure the impact of the remaining disparities in laws, policies, and regulations and in the resources devoted to implementing them. However, when a state such as China seeks to exploit loopholes in or adopt loose interpretations of the NSG guidelines, it threatens to undermine the global nuclear export control regime. Thus, one of the main objectives of the members of the NSG should be to hold China accountable for its exports to Pakistan.

STRENGTHENING SAFEGUARDS. Nuclear-supplier states should ensure that the IAEA has the financial, political, and technical support it needs to implement an effective safeguards system. The NSG could help improve the IAEA safeguards system significantly by requiring the AP as a condition of supply.

PREVENTING THE SPREAD OF ENRICHMENT AND REPROCESSING. Controls on transfers of enrichment and reprocessing should be reinforced with efficient enrichment services, back-up fuel supply assurances, and spent fuel management services.

LIMITING AND ELIMINATING THE USE OF HIGHLY ENRICHED URANIUM. Suppliers should develop technologies that do not rely on HEU for research or medical isotope production. In the meantime, they should adopt export policies that tie the export of HEU to a commitment by the recipient to convert from HEU to low-enriched uranium (LEU) fuel for research reactors and to commit to eliminating HEU from international commerce.

PROMOTING THE UNIVERSALITY OF NUCLEAR TRADE RULES. The United States and other NSG members should persuade all states to abide by the ZC or NSG guidelines and to assist them in implementing adequate export control systems called for by UN Security Council Resolution 1540.

REQUIRING CONSENT RIGHTS OVER ENRICHMENT. The NSG does not now call for a consent right on enrichment. This is an important gap that needs to be filled. NSG members should adopt new language requiring consent rights over enrichment.

REQUIRING PERPETUITY OF ALL NONPROLIFERATION CONTROLS. The NSG should extend its guideline on the perpetuity of international safeguards to all of the nonprolifera-tion controls and guarantees contained in the guidelines.

STRENGTHENING PHYSICAL PROTECTION. The NSG should require recipient states to invite the IAEA to conduct a peer review of their physical protection laws, regulations, and measures.

PREVENTING CLANDESTINE PROCUREMENT. Suppliers must establish adequate export control systems and devote the needed resources to implementing them effectively and share in-formation with each other to prevent clandestine procurements.

UPDATING CONTROL LISTS. The NSG is currently reviewing its control lists, but it needs to update these more frequently to keep up with the rapid pace of technological change.

PROMOTING THE LEGITIMACY OF EXPORT CONTROLS. Suppliers need to convince the international community, particularly developing states, of the necessity of adequate export controls to prevent the spread of nuclear weapons and to enable peaceful nuclear commerce. They should avoid taking initiatives that non-nuclear-weapon states regard as discriminatory such as pressuring them to forswear nuclear capabilities that they regard as a sovereign right and one recognized in the NPT. Instead, they should offer positive incentives to forgo sensitive nuclear fuel-cycle technologies.

None of these steps by themselves will eliminate the proliferation risk of international civil nuclear commerce, but, taken together, they could go a long way toward strengthening the barriers to the misuse of civil nuclear commerce for nuclear explosive purposes.

The Role of the United States

The United States needs to take a leadership role in promoting the initiatives outlined above. The effectiveness of Washington in promoting the international and multilateral nuclear trade controls described in this report was possible in no small part because of the technological and export dominance that the United States enjoyed from the 1950s through at least the 1970s. Over time, the number of suppliers has expanded while the U.S. role in the international nuclear market has declined significantly. Today, the United States is only one among many nuclear suppliers.

To play a leadership role, the United States will need to compete in the international market. Some argue that the strict nonproliferation conditions and unnecessarily burdensome export approval requirements harm U.S. exports. These arguments may have some merit but are not the main reason for the decline in the U.S. share of the international market. Other factors are far more important:

- The inevitable emergence of other suppliers long ago undermined the monopoly of supply that the United States enjoyed in the early days of nuclear energy. The future is likely to see the arrival of even more suppliers.
- The nuclear export industries of other major suppliers have strong governmental and financial support that the U.S. nuclear export industry does not enjoy.
- The United States has not built new domestic nuclear power plants in over 30 years. Countries seeking to develop nuclear power are likely to turn for assistance to those states that have growing domestic nuclear power programs, offer competitive fuel-cycle services, and are supporting the development of advanced technologies.

Overcoming these developments and obstacles will not be easy. Subsidies for U.S. nuclear exports have long been controversial and are likely to become more so in the future, particularly in light of severe constraints on the U.S. budget. Forging alliances with foreign firms as Westinghouse and GE have done with Toshiba and Hitachi may be one avenue for promoting U.S. nuclear exports.

Revitalizing the domestic nuclear industry also faces significant challenges. The low price of natural gas plants and the absence of a national nuclear waste policy will significantly slow the nuclear renaissance, and post-Fukushima public concerns and new safety regulations may create additional brakes on nuclear power plant construction. However, the development of small modular reactors, if they prove economically competitive and meet safety standards, could not only rejuvenate the U.S. domestic nuclear industry but also boost the competiveness of the United

States in the international market, particularly in developing countries. If the General Electric-Hitachi Global Laser Enrichment Uranium Enrichment Facility can satisfy proliferation concerns and meet the economic expectations of its supporters, it could give the United States a strong cost advantage in the global enrichment market. One step the United States could take to strengthen its role in the international market and promote its nonproliferation would be to establish a national nuclear waste program that would allow for taking back at least limited quantities of spent fuel produced from U.S. nuclear exports.

Finally, the U.S. has to avoid overreach in instituting new nuclear export controls such as recent efforts by some in the U.S. Government to press new cooperating partners to forswear what they regard as their rights to enrichment and reprocessing technology.

The controls and influence that come with nuclear trade are only one tool in the U.S. arsenal to prevent the spread of nuclear weapons, but one that Washington can ill afford to let shrink further or wither away.

1 INTRODUCTION

Does peaceful nuclear commerce increase the risk of the proliferation of nuclear weapons? Or can nuclear suppliers use peaceful nuclear cooperation to establish legal, political, and normative barriers to the spread of nuclear weapons? Scholars and policymakers have attempted to answer these questions since the beginning of the nuclear age. The export of nuclear technology by the United States and other suppliers has long been the subject of controversy.[1] One aspect of this issue has been the relative importance of so-called demand side versus supply-side factors in explaining nuclear proliferation. Demand-siders highlight considerations influencing a country's motives for acquiring nuclear weapons such as national security concerns, domestic politics, or national prestige,[2] whereas supply-siders stress technological capabilities and the likelihood that the diffusion of technology makes proliferation more likely. One recent supply-side study concluded that sensitive nuclear assistance—for example, the design and construction of nuclear weapons, the supply of weapons-grade fissile material, or assistance in support for building uranium enrichment or plutonium reprocessing facilities—has been important in aiding countries in acquiring a nuclear-weapons capability.[3] Another supply-side study went further, concluding that all types of civilian nuclear assistance raise the risk of proliferation because the dual-use nature of civil nuclear cooperation provides the know-how and materials necessary for a nuclear-weapons program and helps establish expertise relevant to building a nuclear weapon. It concludes that "all forms of atomic assistance—whether it involves training scientists, supplying reactors, or building fuel fabrication facilities—raise the likelihood that nuclear weapons will spread." [4] Some argue that these concerns call for restraining the worldwide development of nuclear power.[5]

Another view is that the policy of secrecy and denial that the United States pursued in the aftermath of Hiroshima and Nagasaki was a failure and that efforts by the United States and even-

1. See for example, *Atoms for Peace: An Analysis after Thirty Years*, Joseph F. Pilat, Robert E. Pendley, and Charles K. Ebinger, eds. (Boulder, CO: Westview Press, 1985); and *Nuclear Power and the Spread of Nuclear Weapons, Can We Have One without the Other?* (Herndon, VA: Potomac Books, 2002).

2. See for example, Scott D. Sagan, "Why Do States Build Nuclear Weapons? Three Models in Search of a Bomb," *International Security* 21, no.3 (Winter 1996/97): 54–86; George Quester, *The Politics of Nuclear Proliferation* (Baltimore: Johns Hopkins University Press, 1973).

3. Matthew Kroenig, "Importing the Bomb: Sensitive Nuclear Assistance and Nuclear Proliferation," *Journal of Conflict Resolution* (2009): 53, http://jcr.sagepub.com/cgi/content/abstract/53/2/161.

4. Matthew Fuhrmann, "Spreading Temptation: Proliferation and Peaceful Nuclear Cooperation Agreements," *International Security* 34, no. 1 (Summer 2009), http://belfercenter.ksg.harvard.edu/files/IS3401_pp007-041_Fuhrmann.pdf.

5. Victor Gilinsky and Henry Sokolski, "Serious Rules for Nuclear Power without Proliferation," Nonproliferation Education Policy Education Center, May 2012, http://www.npolicy.org/article.php?aid=1177&rt=&key=Serious Rules for Nuclear Power without Proliferation&sec=article&author.

tually others to share the peaceful benefits of nuclear energy under nonproliferation controls and conditions have been instrumental in helping build key elements of the global regime to prevent the spread of nuclear weapons.[6]

Nuclear-weapons proliferation is both a supply-side and a demand-side problem and needs to be viewed both in historical context and against today's international landscape. First, most of the nine countries that possess nuclear weapons today acquired their nuclear arsenals primarily through dedicated military programs, clandestine and illegal procurements, and deliberate assistance from nuclear-weapon states and not through the diversion of imported civil nuclear materials and equipment subject to nonproliferation controls—India being a major exception.[7] Second, sharing the benefits of peaceful nuclear trade provided the leverage to help establish the rules and norms of the nonproliferation regime. Third, much of the proliferation occurred before all the elements of the present global nonproliferation regime were put in place.[8] Fourth, of the 30 countries[9] with nuclear power reactors and the 56 countries[10] with operational research reactors today, only nine states—China, France, India, Israel, North Korea, Pakistan, Russia, the United Kingdom, and the United States—have nuclear weapons, while Iran is widely believed to be developing that capability. The rest are non-nuclear-weapon states that are compliant parties to the NPT. Thus, while international assistance can increase the risks of nuclear proliferation, peaceful nuclear cooperation does not lead inevitably to a spread of nuclear weapons. Most civil nuclear programs are peaceful in nature, and the vast majority of states with such programs are abiding by their nonproliferation commitments. Suppliers have employed their nuclear trade policies as a means of establishing the widely accepted principle that states wishing to take advantage of the peaceful applications of nuclear energy must make effective commitments not to misuse that technology for nonpeaceful or explosive purposes and to accept adequate verification of those commitments.

Nevertheless, there is no question that international nuclear trade has assisted some countries in acquiring a nuclear-weapons capability, particularly in the early days of the nuclear era and especially in the training of scientists and engineers in nuclear-related disciplines. International peaceful nuclear commerce and civil nuclear programs carry with them real risks of diversion to

6. See Pilat, Pendley, and Ebinger, *Atoms for Peace*, particularly essays by Bertrand Goldschmidt, Bertram Wolfe, and Lawrence Scheinman.

7. The United States had a dedicated nuclear weapons program as did the Soviet Union, which also benefited from espionage. The United Kingdom and, less so, France benefited from participation in the Manhattan Project. The Soviet Union deliberately provided assistance to the Chinese nuclear weapons program, and China provided Pakistan with highly enriched uranium and a nuclear-weapon design. Stealing uranium enrichment technology from the Netherlands was also critical to the success of the Pakistani nuclear-weapons program. France deliberately aided the Israeli nuclear-weapons program. Iran obtained its enrichment capability though clandestine procurement efforts. Iran, Iraq, and Syria sought a nuclear-weapons capability largely through clandestine procurement.

8. The United States, Russia, the United Kingdom, France, China, Israel, and India obtained nuclear weapons before the NPT, the ZC, the NSG, and other main elements of the nonproliferation regime were put in place. Only Pakistan and North Korea have acquired such weapons since these institutions were established. Several countries that had nuclear-weapon development programs or nuclear weapons in the past have abandoned them, including Brazil, South Korea, South Africa, and Taiwan. Belarus, Kazakhstan, and Ukraine gave up their nuclear weapons following the dissolution of the Soviet Union. Iraq and Syria had their nascent programs eliminated for them.

9. IAEA, *Nuclear Power Reactors in the World*, 2012 Edition, Reference Data Series No.2, IAEA-RDS-2/32 http://www-pub.iaea.org/MTCD/Publications/PDF/RDS2-32_web.pdf.

10. http://www.iaea.org/About/Policy/GC/GC48/Documents/gc48inf-4_ftn1.pdf.

nuclear weapons. Among other things, reactor-grade plutonium produced in nuclear power plants is usable in nuclear weapons; enrichment and reprocessing facilities can produce weapons-usable nuclear materials that are vulnerable to diversion by both states and subnational actors for purposes of building nuclear explosives; and reprocessing plants are difficult and expensive to safeguard. In addition, states can try to use peaceful nuclear cooperation as a means of acquiring skills for developing nuclear weapons. Nuclear-weapon aspirants have also justified their purchases on the international market for their peaceful nuclear programs as a cover for developing a nuclear-weapons capability. Iraq sought to exploit a peaceful nuclear research program to realize its nuclear-weapons ambitions by purchasing a research reactor from France and sensitive research facilities from Italy in the 1970s. Brazil, Iran, Iraq, Pakistan, South Korea, North Korea, and Taiwan have at one time or another cited their peaceful nuclear programs as justification, however implausible, for acquiring sensitive nuclear technologies. States with civil nuclear power programs could also divert material or equipment received from suppliers to nuclear explosives. India violated the nonproliferation commitments it made to Canada and the United States in order to use the facilities and materials it imported from those countries in its nuclear explosives program. Over the past two decades, the IAEA has found Iran, Iraq, Libya, North Korea, Romania, and Syria in noncompliance with their safeguards agreements with the IAEA.

In addition, suppliers have not always acted responsibly. In the 1960s, Canada exported large research reactors, which were ideal for producing weapons-grade plutonium, to both India and Taiwan (then the Republic of China), while France and Germany sought to export reprocessing plants to South Korea, Taiwan, and Pakistan in the 1970s. Even though these exports were under some nonproliferation controls or were intended to be, the exports of these technologies were imprudent.

Wherever one stands on the relative risks and benefits of civil nuclear trade, nuclear power and civil nuclear trade are unlikely to disappear. These risks must be taken into account as we look to the future of nuclear energy. Nuclear power continues to help meet the electricity needs of many countries around the globe, and it is likely to grow as countries adopt more stringent carbon dioxide emission policies. Despite the Fukushima accident in Japan and the resulting concerns about the safety of nuclear energy, a recent report by the World Energy Council stated that at least 50 countries are building, operating, or considering nuclear power as part of their energy mix.[11] The IAEA has projected that, by the year 2035,the world's capacity for generating electricity through nuclear power will grow from 375 GWe net (at the end of 2010) to between 540 GWe net in the low-demand case and 746 GWe net in the high-demand case, increases of 44 percent and 99 percent, respectively.[12] At the 2012 IAEA General Conference, the agency released its updated high and low projections for the world's nuclear power generating capacity. According to the report, "In the 2012 updated low projection, the world's installed nuclear power capacity grows from 370 gigawatts today to 456 GW(e) in 2030, diminishing by 9 percent from the level projected last year. In the updated high projection, it grows to 740 GW(e) in 2030, which is an increase that is about 1 percent less than estimated in 2011."[13] These numbers show a decrease in the agency's 2011 projections but underline the fact that nuclear power will remain an important option for many countries, with developing countries continuing to show a strong interest in nuclear power.

---

11. *World Energy Perspective: Nuclear Energy One Year after Fukushima*, World Energy Council, 2011, http://www.worldenergy.org/documents/world_energy_perspective__nuclear_energy_one_year_after_fukushima_world_energy_council_march_2012_1.pdf.

12. IAEA, "Global Uranium Supply Ensured for Long Term," news release 2012/19, New Report Shows, July 16, 2012, http://www.iaea.org/newscenter/pressreleases/2012/prn201219.html.

13. "The IAEA Updates Its Projections for Nuclear Power in 2030," September 25, 2012, http://www.iaea.org/newscenter/news/2012/np2030.html.

In addition, the International Energy Agency (IEA) has estimated that the world's nuclear power capacity needs to nearly double by 2025 to help meet climate targets.[14] Today, only a few states are known to be seeking nuclear weapons. However, this may change as more countries develop nuclear power, seek sensitive nuclear capabilities, and face security threats they believe can be addressed through acquisition of nuclear weapons. In particular, Iran's acquisition of nuclear weapons could demonstrate a proliferation pathway for other states within the NPT. Therefore, one of the key challenges that the nonproliferation regime faces is to ensure that the projected growth in, and spread of, commercial nuclear power, if actually realized, will take place under conditions that provide the maximum protection against the misuse of civil nuclear technology for military or nuclear explosives purposes. Thus, requiring strict nonproliferation conditions on peaceful nuclear trade must remain an indispensable part of any nonproliferation strategy. The United States has an important role to play in ensuring that the rules of international nuclear trade keep pace with the proliferation challenges in the years ahead.

Such trade began with the Atoms for Peace Program in the 1950s when the United States concluded civil nuclear cooperation agreements with a number of states interested in exploiting the peaceful benefits of nuclear energy. In these agreements, the United States required recipients to give peaceful-use assurances and accept inspections on imported nuclear items as well as other nonproliferation controls as conditions of supply on nuclear materials, reactors, and fuel-cycle services.

Until the early 1970s, the United States was the dominant supplier in the international commercial nuclear market. As other advanced nuclear states entered the global marketplace, they too entered into bilateral nuclear supply agreements with the growing number of countries that were then interested in applications of civil nuclear power. The export control policies of these suppliers varied in scope and nature. The bilateral controls of individual supplier states were eventually supplemented by two internationally coordinated nuclear export control regimes. The first—known as the Zangger Committee—was established in 1974 to implement article III.2 of the Treaty on the Non-Proliferation of Nuclear Weapons, which obliges states that are party to the treaty to require IAEA safeguards on their export of nuclear materials and equipment. The members of the ZC, which now number 38, defined the specific nuclear materials and equipment that were only generally identified in article III.2 of the treaty and placed these items on a "Trigger List," so called because the export of listed items "triggered" certain conditions of supply, including the acceptance of safeguards by the IAEA on nuclear exports as well as peaceful, nonexplosive-use assurances by recipient states that were not party to the NPT (see IAEA document INFCIRC/209).

The second multilateral arrangement is the 46-member Nuclear Suppliers Group. The NSG adopted nuclear export guidelines[15] in response to several nonproliferation crises in the 1970s: the detonation of a nuclear explosive device by India and the efforts by some supplier states to export reprocessing technology to Brazil, Pakistan, South Korea, and Taiwan and, in the case of Brazil, both enrichment and reprocessing technology. All of these countries lacked any credible peaceful justification for the acquisition of such sensitive nuclear technologies and had nuclear-weapons

14. International Energy Agency, "Tracking Clean Energy Progress: Energy Technology Perspectives 2012," excerpt as IEA input to the Clean Energy Ministerial, 2012," http://www.iea.org/media/etp/Tracking_Clean_Energy_Progress.pdf.

15. IAEA Information Circular (INFCIRC/254), "Communication Received from Certain Member States Regarding Guidelines for the Export of Nuclear Material, Equipment or Technology," February 1978, Part 2, http://www.iaea.org/Publications/Documents/Infcircs/Others/infcirc254.shtml.

ambitions or actual programs. The NSG adopted the ZC Trigger List of nuclear items but also agreed to apply conditions to nuclear exports that went beyond the requirements of the NPT and the ZC and included assurances of adequate physical protection and special restraints on the export of sensitive nuclear technology. These guidelines have evolved over time to include, among other things, additional nonproliferation conditions and controls on the export of dual-use items.[16]

In addition to these multilateral arrangements, the members of the European Atomic Energy Community[17] as well as the major holders of plutonium have adopted guidelines on certain nuclear transfers. In 1984, the European Community adopted its "Declaration of Common Policy," published as INFCIRC/322,[18] that set forth guidelines for the transfer and retransfer of plutonium, highly enriched uranium, and sensitive nuclear technology, facilities, and equipment among member states. In 1997, Belgium, China, Germany, Japan, the Russian Federation, Switzerland, the United Kingdom, and the United States published "Guidelines on the Management of Plutonium" (INFCIRC/549), which, among other things, specified certain conditions that would govern their international transfers of separated plutonium.[19]

In 2004, the UN Security Council adopted Resolution 1540, which calls on states to put in place "appropriate effective measures to account for and secure" items related to the production, use, storage, or transport of weapons of mass destruction and their means of delivery and to "maintain appropriate effective physical protection measures" of said items. The primary purpose was to deny such items to nonstate actors, but it also obliges states to establish effective export controls.[20]

This report examines the role of nuclear export controls in reducing the risk that international nuclear commerce will be misused for nuclear explosive purposes. The report has several aims:

- To describe the specific nonproliferation assurances and conditions that the United States requires in its nuclear export policies
- To explain the importance of each of these controls in minimizing the risks that nuclear exports will be used for explosive or military purposes
- To compare the nature and scope of U.S. nonproliferation controls with those of the nuclear export policies of other exporting states as reflected in the guidelines of such multilateral arrangements as the ZC, the NSG, and other international agreements and understandings, and, where known, the specific export policies of other individual nuclear-supplier states

---

16. Ibid.

17. The treaty establishing the European Atomic Energy Community coordinates research, safety standards, and investment to promote peaceful uses of atomic energy in the European Union. It includes a common market for specialized material and equipment and ensures its members supply of nuclear fuel and ores, functionally creating a centralized system for supply and funding of European nuclear energy activities. See "Treaty Establishing the European Atomic Energy Community," March 25, 1957, 298 U.N.T.S., 167, available at eur-lex.europa.eu.

18. IAEA Information Circular (INFCIRC/322), "Communication Received from the Resident Representative of Italy on Behalf of the European Community," April 1985, http://www.iaea.org/Publications/Documents/Infcircs/Others/inf322.shtml.

19. IAEA Information Circular (INFCIRC/549/Add, 8), "Communication Received from Certain Member States Concerning their Policies Regarding the Management of Plutonium," March 31, 1998, http://www.iaea.org/Publications/Documents/Infcircs/1998/infcirc549a8.pdf.

20. United Nations Resolution 1540 (April 28, 2004).

- To assess the limits, weaknesses, and strengths as well as the successes and failures of U.S. nuclear export controls and those of other nuclear suppliers to date
- To identify the challenges for the future and the role that the United States should play in meeting these challenges.

2 NONPROLIFERATION CONTROLS AND GUARANTEES: A COMPARISON

The United States and other major nuclear suppliers generally require non-nuclear-weapon states to provide a number of assurances as a condition of nuclear cooperation. They also require certain assurances from nuclear-weapon states, but these are less comprehensive than those from non-nuclear-weapon states. Assurances include government-to-government guarantees of nonexplosive use, acceptance of IAEA safeguards, guarantees of establishing effective physical protection on nuclear materials, controls on the transfer of sensitive nuclear technologies (enrichment and reprocessing), and requirements that recipient governments obtain the prior consent of the supplier state before retransferring nuclear materials and equipment to third states, reprocessing, alteration in form or content or enrichment of nuclear materials, and the storage of weapons-usable materials. Suppliers also provide for the termination of nuclear cooperation if a recipient state violates its nonproliferation commitments. In addition, the major suppliers institute controls on the export of specified dual-use items, for example, those that have both nuclear and nonnuclear uses, as well as "catch-all controls" on items even if they are not on any export control list but are intended for use in a nuclear explosive device.

The following sections compare the various nonproliferation assurances, controls, and conditions the United States requires for its nuclear exports with those of key international or multinational nonproliferation arrangements, treaties, and conventions and, where known, those required by other individual nuclear suppliers.

In this comparison, several important facts are noteworthy:

- The U.S. Atomic Energy Act (AEA)[21] requires that special nuclear material and nuclear facilities and their major nuclear components may be exported only pursuant to an agreement for cooperation.[22] Other nuclear components and substances can be exported

21. U.S. Atomic Energy Act of 1954 (as amended though P.L. 105-394, November 13, 1998), http//: uscode.house.gov/.

22. *Special nuclear material* is defined as plutonium, uranium enriched in the isotope 233 or in the isotope 235, or any other material that the Nuclear Regulatory Commission determines to be special nuclear material. These are materials deemed most directly relevant for use in nuclear weapons. In addition, since the enactment of the NNPA, the U.S. government has consistently required that an agreement for cooperation be in place for any commercial exports of source material. This practice is supported by section 402 of the Nuclear Non-Proliferation Act, which prohibits the export of source material for purposes of enrichment except pursuant to an agreement for cooperation. (Source material includes uranium, thorium, or any other material that the NRC determines by regulation to be source material or ores containing one or more of the foregoing materials in such concentration as the NRC may determine from time to time.) Nuclear equipment includes (1) "utilization facilities," including power and research reactors and the four major components of these reactors (pressure vessels, the primary coolant pumps, the complete control rod system, and, in the case of heavy water reactors, the fuel charging and discharging machines); and (2) "produc-

without such an agreement. Section 109 (b) of the AEA requires that recipients of these components and substances agree to accept the application of safeguards to such items, provide an assurance of peaceful, nonexplosive use, and agree not to retransfer such items to other countries without U.S. prior consent. In addition to the requirements of section 104, the export of such components and substances must also satisfy the guidelines of the NSG.

- The description of the nonproliferation controls contained in U.S. peaceful nuclear cooperation agreements applies to agreements that have entered into effect after the enactment of the Nuclear Non-Proliferation Act of 1978, which amended the Atomic Energy Act to include a range of new nonproliferation assurances and controls.[23]
- Not all U.S. agreements for peaceful nuclear cooperation are the same. Although almost all contain the nonproliferation controls required by U.S. law, they vary in the way these are implemented, depending on the nature of the relationship of the United States with a cooperating partner, the state of its civil nuclear program, and the proliferation risks involved in peaceful nuclear trade with the particular country or region where it is located.
- U.S. agreements for peaceful nuclear cooperation are not commitments to supply nuclear materials, equipment, components, or technology. They provide only the legal framework for such nuclear exports, and U.S. nuclear exports require a license from the U.S. Nuclear Regulatory Commission (NRC) and must satisfy the U.S. nuclear export criteria set forth in sections 127 and 128 of the AEA. (These criteria generally track the conditions and controls required for agreements of cooperation by section 123 of the AEA.) The Department of Energy authorizes the export of nuclear technology. The Department of Commerce licenses the export of all items other than those licensed by the NRC, which, if used for purposes other than those for which the export is intended, could be of significance for nuclear explosive purposes, such as dual-use exports.

---

tion facilities," including reactors for producing nuclear material through irradiation, as well as enrichment and reprocessing plants and important component parts especially designed for such facilities.

23. Two agreements—with South Korea and Taiwan – predate the NNPA, have not yet been amended to meet the requirements of the NNPA, and do not include all the controls required by the NNPA. The United States has had to obtain separate assurances from Taiwan and South Korea in order to license nuclear exports from the United States. For example, both agreements prohibit the use of items subject to the agreement for atomic weapons, but not nuclear explosive devices. In the case of Taiwan, the United States obtained a separate assurance on nuclear explosive devices. The United States also obtained separate assurances from South Korea and Taiwan for physical protection. Neither South Korea nor Taiwan has been willing to renegotiate their agreements with the U.S. to bring them into conformity with the NNPA. However, the U.S. agreements with South Korea and Taiwan will expire in the year 2014, and their replacements will have to conform to the requirements of the NNPA. Pursuant to section 6 of the Taiwan Relations Act, P.L. 96-8, 93 Stat. 14, and Executive Order 12143, 44 F.R. 37191, all agreements concluded with the Taiwan authorities prior to January 1, 1979 are administered on a nongovernmental basis by the American Institute in Taiwan, a nonprofit District of Columbia corporation, and constitute neither recognition of Taiwan authorities nor the continuation of any official relationship with Taiwan.

- Not all nonproliferation conditions contained in U.S. agreements for peaceful nuclear cooperation are required by law. [24] Some are conditions of U.S. policy. Examples include fall-back safeguards and the Additional Protocol.
- The materials, equipment, and technology subject to U.S. export controls are the same as those specified in the Trigger Lists of nuclear materials and items and the dual-use lists of the ZC and the NSG.
- While the major nonproliferation treaties and conventions such as the NPT and the Convention on the Physical Protection of Nuclear Materials impose legal obligations on their parties, the understandings of the ZC and the NSG are not legally binding commitments but voluntary guidelines. Nevertheless, the states adhering to these guidelines have indicated that they would act in accordance with the guidelines.
- The ZC and the NSG neither deny nor approve exports. Each adhering state approves or denies license applications in accordance with its own national export laws, regulations, and policies, but these are based on common conditions of supply and principles voluntarily agreed to in multilateral arrangements.
- While most U.S. nonproliferation requirements are set out in U.S. law and export regulations and the texts of U.S. agreements for peaceful nuclear cooperation are published, many suppliers are not as open in disclosing the details of their peaceful nuclear cooperation agreements, the specific nonproliferation undertakings they require, or the precise way in which they implement them. Although the major suppliers adhere to the same guidelines of the ZC and the NSG, some variation exists among individual supplier policies, practices, and interpretation of the international guidelines.

---

24. U.S. peaceful nuclear cooperation agreements are often referred to as "123" agreements because the main legal requirements for such agreements are found in section 123 of the Atomic Energy Act. However, this is an inapt and too narrow a label for such agreements since they contain nonproliferation controls and conditions that are specified in other sections of the Atomic Energy Act and the Nuclear Non-Proliferation Act as well as U.S. policy and practices that go beyond the strict requirements of U.S. law.

Peaceful, Nonexplosive Use Guarantees

View of the Asco Nuclear Power Plant in Spain. Credit: Carles Torras 2008. http://www.flickr.com/photos/carlesviana/2964902602/.

A state's legally binding assurance that the materials and equipment it imports from a nuclear supplier will not be used to develop nuclear explosives is the most basic nonproliferation commitment. This obligation is indispensable in ensuring that international civil nuclear commerce will be confined to peaceful applications of nuclear energy and will not be diverted to explosive uses. The importance of explicitly prohibiting the use of imported nuclear materials and equipment not only for nuclear weapons but also for nuclear explosives is illustrated by India's exploitation of vague Canadian and U.S. "peaceful-use" supply conditions to divert nuclear supplies from these countries to manufacture what New Delhi claimed was a "peaceful" nuclear explosive device.

In the early days of the nuclear era, suppliers insisted that their nuclear exports be used only for peaceful purposes and not for "atomic weapons" and did not explicitly include a prohibition on the use of such supplied items for nuclear explosive devices. This omission led to a major diversion of peaceful nuclear trade for nuclear-weapons purposes. In the 1960s, the Indians bought a heavy water research reactor from Canada and leased heavy water from the United States that it used to produce the plutonium for its first nuclear explosion in 1974. Both the research reactor and the heavy water were supplied on the condition that they be used only for peaceful purposes but were not subject to either bilateral inspections or IAEA safeguards. The Indians claimed that their 1974 test was of a peaceful nuclear device, not a nuclear weapon, and that they were in compliance with the peaceful-use assurances that they had provided to the suppliers. However, neither the United States nor Canada agreed with this interpretation,[25] nor did they accept the proposition that there was any meaningful distinction between a peaceful nuclear device and a nuclear weapon.

25. In fact, both suppliers made this position clear in written communications to the Indian government prior to the test.

UNITED STATES. The Atomic Energy Act 123(a) (3) requires a guarantee by the cooperating party that "no nuclear materials and equipment or sensitive nuclear technology to be transferred pursuant to such agreement, and no special nuclear material produced through the use of any nuclear materials and equipment or sensitive nuclear technology transferred pursuant to such agreement will be used for any nuclear explosive device, or for research on or development of any nuclear explosive device, or for any other military purpose."[26] Note that the nuclear material identified above will hereafter be referred to as "U.S.-obligated" or "material subject to the agreement." These terms cover not only the nuclear material and equipment that the United States supplies directly to another country but also the material used in or produced through the use of U.S.-supplied nuclear materials and equipment. For example, if non-U.S.-supplied material is irradiated in a U.S.-supplied reactor, that material will be subject to all the terms and conditions of the U.S. agreement. The United States also views this prohibition as applying to any subsequent generations of plutonium.

TREATIES AND INTERNATIONAL AGREEMENTS

Treaty on the Non-Proliferation of Nuclear Weapons. Article II of the treaty provides that each non-nuclear-weapon state that is party to the treaty undertakes not to receive the transfer from any transferor whatsoever of nuclear weapons or other nuclear explosive devices or of control over such weapons or explosive devices directly, or indirectly; not to manufacture or otherwise acquire nuclear weapons or other nuclear explosive devices; and not to seek or receive any assistance in the manufacture of nuclear weapons or other nuclear explosive devices.

The NPT does not ban nonexplosive military uses and allows for the withdrawal of nuclear material from safeguards, for example, for naval propulsion. According to the model NPT safeguards agreement (INFCIRC/153), a state withdrawing material for nonexplosive military use must inform the agency that the use of the material in a nonproscribed military activity will not conflict with any peaceful-use pledge the state may have given; and when material has been withdrawn from safeguards, that state must not use it for nuclear weapons or other nuclear explosive devices. This withdrawal provision has never been used.

Article II of the IAEA Statute bans the use of any Agency assistance from furthering any military purpose. In addition, the IAEA's non-NPT safeguards agreements, so-called INFIRC/66 Rev. 2 safeguards agreement establish a system of controls to enable the Agency to comply with this statutory obligation.

Nuclear-Weapon-Free-Zone Treaties. The Treaty of Tlatelolco (Latin America), the Treaty of Rarotonga (South Pacific), the Bangkok Treaty (Southeast Asia), and the Pelindaba Treaty all contain nonexplosive use assurances but do not ban nonexplosive military uses.

Zangger Committee and NSG. The ZC guidelines provide that exports to a non-nuclear-weapon state not party to the treaty should require a guarantee by the recipient government that source or special fissionable material transferred, or produced, processed, or

26. The AEA exempts agreements specifically for the military applications of atomic energy (Sec 91 c).

used in the facility for which the transferred item is intended, shall not be diverted to nuclear weapons or other nuclear explosive devices. The Zangger Committee does not ban the use of Trigger-List items for military purposes. The NSG guidelines require "formal governmental assurances from recipients explicitly excluding uses which would result in any nuclear explosive device."

U.S. law bans any country from using materials, equipment, and technology that it imports from the United States for any military purpose. International treaties and agreements (the NPT, ZC, and NSG) do not, but the IAEA statute bans the use of agency assistance from furthering any military purpose. The NSG guidelines apply to "nuclear transfers for peaceful purposes to any non-nuclear-weapon state." They do not apply to civil transfers to nuclear-weapon states. However, other suppliers as a matter of policy often include a no-military-use pledge in their bilateral agreements.

The U.S. ban on the "research on or development of" as well as use of nuclear explosives and any military use of any item subject to a U.S. agreement for peaceful nuclear cooperation is more detailed, specific, and comprehensive than that found in the NPT ("the manufacture or acquisition" of nuclear explosives), the ZC (the "diversion to nuclear weapons or other nuclear explosives"), or the NSG ("uses which would result in any nuclear explosive device.") However, the differences in these formulations do not appear to have had any practical implications to date.

Safeguards

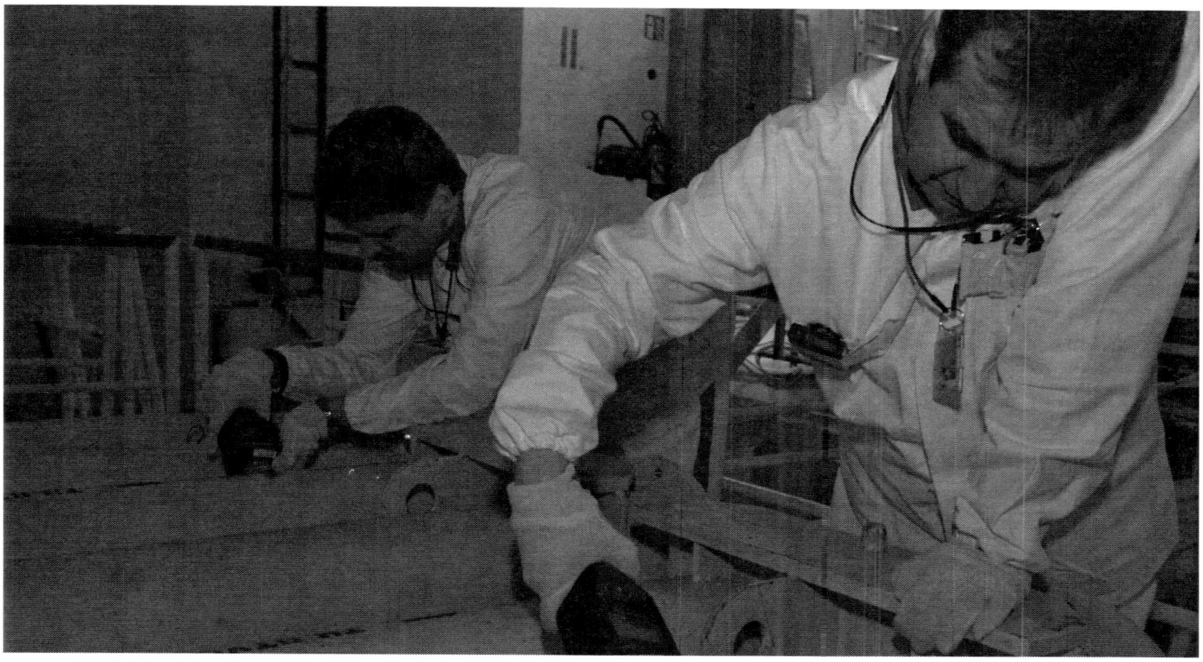

Scenes from a verification training exercise. IAEA safeguards inspector using HM-5 devices to check the presence of fuel assembly in a transport container located in the fresh fuel storage of the Mochovce Nuclear Power Plant. Credit: Dean Calma/IAEA 2005. http://www.iaea.org/NewsCenter/Multimedia/Imagebank/index.jsp.

The objective of international safeguards, which are administered by the IAEA,[27] is "the timely detection of diversion of significant quantities of nuclear material from peaceful nuclear activities to the manufacture of nuclear weapons or of other nuclear explosive devices or for purposes unknown, and the deterrence of such diversion by the threat of early detection."[28] Requiring acceptance of IAEA safeguards on peaceful nuclear activities as a condition of nuclear supply is essential to verifying the basic nonproliferation commitment that importing states make to abstain from using their civil nuclear program for nuclear weapons or nuclear explosives. There are several aspects to the requirement for safeguards as a condition of nuclear supply that merit attention: safeguards on exported nuclear materials and equipment (an NPT obligation required of nuclear suppliers for their nuclear exports to non-NPT parties); comprehensive safeguards on all the peaceful nuclear activities of non-nuclear-weapon states; perpetuity of safeguards; fall-back safeguards; the Additional Protocol to a state's safeguards agreement; and safeguards in nuclear-weapon states.

---

27. EURATOM administers its own safeguards systems in member states of the EU. EURATOM and the IAEA have entered into an agreement that provides for a division of labor in the administration of safeguards between the two organizations. In addition, a Common System of Accounting and Control of Nuclear Material (SCCC) was established by Argentina and Brazil in July 1992. It is a full scope safeguards system in both countries. The Brazilian-Argentine Agency for Accounting and Control of Nuclear Materials (ABACC) was created to apply the SCCC.

28. IAEA Information Circular (INFCIRC/153[Corrected]), "The Struggle and Content of Agreements between the Agency and States Required in Connection with the Treaty on the Nonproliferation of Nuclear Weapons," June 1972, paragraph 28, http://www.iaea.org/Publications/Documents/Infcircs/Others/infcirc153.pdf .

Comprehensive Safeguards in Non-Nuclear-Weapon States

Until the late 1970s, supplier states required safeguards only on their exports of nuclear material and equipment as required by the NPT. Beginning in the late 1970s, the United States and a few other nuclear-exporting states began to insist that recipients accept safeguards on all their peaceful nuclear activities as a condition of nuclear supply—comprehensive or full-scope safeguards. Without such a requirement, a nonparty to the NPT could import nuclear materials and equipment under safeguards but still pursue a parallel, unsafeguarded nuclear program for nuclear explosive purposes. Such a state could thereby enjoy the benefits of international peaceful commerce while keeping its options open for a nuclear-weapons program. Requiring comprehensive safeguards as a condition of supply closes this legal loophole.

UNITED STATES. The AEA 123 (a) (2) requires, as a condition of continued U.S. nuclear supply, that IAEA safeguards be maintained with respect to all nuclear materials in all peaceful nuclear activities within the territory of a non-nuclear-weapon state and in territory under its jurisdiction or in peaceful nuclear activities carried out under its control anywhere.

All U.S. post-NNPA agreements for peaceful nuclear cooperation with non-nuclear-weapon states contain a comprehensive safeguards requirement except for the U.S. agreement with India. The administration of George W. Bush did not include the comprehensive IAEA safeguards requirement in the U.S. nuclear cooperation agreement with India, even though New Delhi is not a nuclear-weapon state as defined by the NPT. Congress approved this agreement in 2008, thus reversing a decades-long U.S. nonproliferation policy.

TREATIES AND INTERNATIONAL AGREEMENTS

Treaty on the Non-Proliferation of Nuclear Weapons. The treaty requires all non-nuclear-weapon states parties to accept safeguards on all source and special fissionable material in all their peaceful nuclear activities. However, as noted above, it does not require suppliers to impose comprehensive safeguards as a condition of nuclear supply to non-nuclear-weapon states not party to the treaty. It requires suppliers to place safeguards only on their exports of nuclear materials and nuclear equipment to such states. The 1995 NPT Review and Extension Conference endorsed comprehensive safeguards as a condition of new supply arrangements, and the 2010 NPT Review Conference reiterated the 1995 statement, thus enhancing comprehensive safeguards as a broadly accepted international norm.

Zangger Committee and Nuclear Suppliers Group. The ZC implements the NPT in requiring safeguards only on members' exports and re-exports of nuclear materials and equipment to non-nuclear-weapon states not party to the treaty.

In 1993, NSG members agreed that they would supply Trigger-List items only if the recipient non-nuclear-weapon state had a comprehensive safeguards agreement with the IAEA. However, the new NSG guideline was neither absolute nor without exception since it contained two significant loopholes. First, it applied only to new nuclear supply commitments, thus exempting existing commitments (the so-called grandfather clause).[29]

---

29. By contrast, the NNPA requirement for comprehensive safeguards is retroactive and thus applied to U.S. nuclear cooperation agreements entered into before 1980. This resulted in the cutoff of U.S. nuclear cooperation with such states as Argentina, Brazil, India, and Pakistan beginning in 1980.

Second, the NSG guideline contained a "safety exception," which specified that transfers of Trigger-List items without the comprehensive safeguards requirement "should only be authorized in exceptional cases when they are deemed essential for the safe operation of existing facilities and if safeguards are applied to those facilities."

UN Security Council Resolution 1887. Resolution 1887, which the UN Security Council adopted in 2009,[30] called on all non-nuclear-weapon states party to the NPT that have yet to bring into force a comprehensive safeguards agreement to do so immediately.

Other States. The United States was not the first supplier to adopt a requirement for comprehensive safeguards. A few suppliers preceded the United States in imposing this condition of supply: Canada in 1976, Australia and Sweden in 1977, and Poland and Czechoslovakia in 1978. Japan and Germany followed in 1989 and 1990, respectively.

The disparities that existed until 1993 in the policies of major suppliers on comprehensive safeguards had important implications. The failure of all members of the NSG to adopt comprehensive safeguards meant that countries such as Argentina, Brazil, and India were able to obtain nuclear supplies from states such as West Germany, Switzerland, and France, while carrying on parallel nuclear-weapons programs or resisting safeguards on all their nuclear activities.

The "grandfather" and "safety" exceptions of the NSG guidelines have undermined the comprehensive safeguards norm. Russia used both exceptions as justification for its nuclear exports to India. China has cited the grandfather clause as an excuse for its nuclear cooperation with Pakistan. India and Pakistan are two non-NPT parties that do not accept IAEA safeguards on all their nuclear activities. Also damaging to the comprehensive safeguards norm was the U.S. initiative to carve out an exception for India from this NSG condition of supply.

The NSG adoption of comprehensive safeguards in 1993 as a condition of nuclear supply to non-nuclear-weapon states removed the disparity in supplier policies and made the comprehensive safeguards export requirement a general international norm. However, that norm has been seriously undercut by the actions of such suppliers as China, Russia, and the United States.

30. On September 24, 2009, U.S. President Barack Obama chaired a meeting of the UN Security Council (UNSC) that unanimously adopted Resolution 1887 (2009) on nonproliferation and disarmament. The resolution, which was drafted at an initiative of the Obama Administration and which was the result of months of negotiations, sets forth a series of goals to eliminate nuclear weapons, ban production of the fissile material for nuclear weapons, and prohibit all nuclear weapons tests and protect stockpiles of weapons-usable nuclear materials.

Perpetuity of Safeguards

The objective of perpetuity of safeguards on nuclear materials is to ensure that safeguards continue to apply to nuclear materials even if a cooperation agreement or a treaty expires or is terminated or suspended. The principle of perpetuity of safeguards is based on IAEA safeguards standards and practice. Paragraph 11 of IAEA document INFCIRC/153 (the IAEA model NPT safeguards agreement) states that an NPT safeguards agreement should provide that safeguards on nuclear material subject to safeguards shall terminate "upon determination by the Agency that... [such material] has been consumed, or has been diluted in such a way that it is no longer usable for any nuclear activity relevant from the point of view of safeguards, or has become practicably irrecoverable." In other words, safeguards must continue to be applied until the nuclear material is no longer usable or cannot be recovered, for example, when minute quantities are embedded in nuclear waste. In addition, Gov. 1621 adopted by the IAEA Board of Governors in 1973 states that the provisions for terminating a non-NPT safeguards agreement (INFCIRC/66/Rev.2) "should be formulated in such a way that the rights and obligations of the parties continue to apply in connection with supplied nuclear material and with special fissionable material produced, processed or used in or in connection with supplied nuclear material, equipment, facilities or non-nuclear material, until such time as the Agency has terminated the application of safeguards thereto, in accordance with the provisions of paragraph 26 or 27 of the Agency's Safeguarded System."

UNITED STATES. The AEA, section 123 (a) (1), requires a guarantee by the cooperating party that safeguards as set forth in the agreement for cooperation will be maintained with respect to all U.S.-obligated nuclear materials and equipment, so long as they remain under the jurisdiction or control of the cooperating party, irrespective of the duration of other provisions in the agreement or whether the agreement is terminated or suspended for any reason. Thus, even if a U.S. agreement with a cooperating partner is terminated or expires or if the cooperating partner withdraws from the NPT, safeguards must continue to apply to items subject to the agreement.

TREATIES AND INTERNATIONAL AGREEMENTS

Treaty on the Non-Proliferation of Nuclear Weapons. Article X, paragraph 1, of the treaty provides that a state party to the treaty has the right to withdraw from it if it decides that extraordinary events, related to the subject matter of the treaty, have jeopardized its supreme interests. The model NPT safeguards agreement (INFCIRC/153) provides that such an agreement is to "remain in force as long as the State is party to the [NPT]."[31] Thus, if a non-nuclear-weapon state validly withdraws from the NPT, its safeguards agreement would no longer be in force. This provision contrasts with safeguards agreements by non-NPT parties (INFCIRC/66) that require safeguards in perpetuity. However, while not removing this distinction between parties and nonparties to the NPT, the decision in 1995 to extend the NPT indefinitely has helped promote the principle of perpetuity of safeguards.

Nuclear Suppliers Group. The guidelines also contain a requirement for perpetuity of safeguards, but it does not apply to supply contracts with non-nuclear-weapon states concluded before April 3, 1992.

Nuclear-Weapon-Free-Zone Treaties and Regional Arrangements. The Treaty of Tlatelolco (Latin America), the Raratonga Treaty (South Pacific), the Bangkok Treaty (South-

31. IAEA Information Circular (INFCIRC/153[Corrected]), paragraph 26, http://www.iaea.org/Publications/Documents/Infcircs/Others/infcirc153.pdf .

east Asia), and the Pelindaba Treaty all contain peaceful-use and safeguards provisions that are independent of NPT membership.[32] However, the most recent such treaty, the Central Asian Nuclear-Weapon-Free-Zone Treaty, refers specifically to application of safeguards pursuant to the NPT. The EURATOM Treaty, which predates the NPT, establishes a regional safeguards system. Thus, a sizable number of states have already undertaken peaceful-use and safeguards commitments that would endure regardless of their adherence to the NPT. However, a state withdrawing from the NPT may also seek to withdraw from other relevant treaties.

UN Security Council Resolution 1887. Resolution 1887 urges all states to require, as a condition of export, that recipients allow for continuation of safeguards on any received nuclear material and equipment, even if they have terminated their IAEA safeguards agreement. This would also apply to any special nuclear material produced through the use of such material or equipment.

A requirement for perpetuity of safeguards is now widely accepted international practice among suppliers. However, the ability of a state to withdraw from the NPT and terminate its comprehensive safeguards agreement with the IAEA remains an important loophole as illustrated by the actions of North Korea when it expelled agency inspectors in 2002 and withdrew from the NPT in 2003.

Additional Protocol

As a result of the failure of the IAEA to detect Iraq's massive nuclear-weapons program before 1991, the IAEA Board of Governors in 1997 approved the Model Additional Protocol (INFCIRC/540)[33] to its safeguards agreements to improve its authority to detect clandestine nuclear activities. Under the NPT safeguard agreements (INFCIRC/153), inspectors' rights of access are limited. For routine inspections, they are limited to key measuring points in declared facilities. The IAEA had the right to conduct so-called special inspections, if it considered that information provided by a state was not adequate for it to fulfill its safeguards responsibilities, and it had the right to gain access to information and locations beyond those specified in the safeguards agreement. However, in practice the agency inspectors had largely confined themselves to inspecting only declared facilities up to 1991. The weaknesses in this approach became readily apparent as the extent of Iraq's nuclear-weapons program and activities at undeclared facilities was revealed.

The AP expands the agency's authority and practices to gain increased information about and access to a state's nuclear activities and thereby greatly enhances its ability to detect illegal, clan-

32. John Carlson, "NPT Withdrawal: Consequences for IAEA Safeguards" (ICNND Research Paper 8, International Commission on Nuclear Non-proliferation and Disarmament, Canberra, 2009), http://icnnd.org/documents/carlson_npt_withdrawal.pdf .

33. IAEA Information Circular (INFCIRC/540 [Corrected]), "Model Protocol Additional to the Agreement(s) between State(s) and the International Atomic Energy Agency for the Application of Safeguards," http://www.iaea.org/Publications/Documents/Infcircs/1997/infcirc540c.pdf.

destine activities.[34] In combination with a comprehensive safeguards agreement, the AP provides a picture of a state's holdings of nuclear material and fuel-cycle activities that is as complete as practical and is a necessary tool for uncovering illegal, clandestine nuclear activities.

UNITED STATES. U.S. law does not require the Additional Protocol as a condition of U.S. nuclear supply under peaceful nuclear cooperation agreements. However, since the IAEA adoption of the Model Additional Protocol in 1997, the United States has included the AP as a condition of supply in its agreements with the Russian Federation (2010), India (2008), and the UAE (2009). Other agreements that entered into force after 1997—Argentina (1997), Australia (2010), Bangladesh (2000), Brazil (1999), Kazakhstan (1999), Morocco (2002), Turkey (2008), and Ukraine (1999)—do not contain a provision on the Additional Protocol. Most cooperating U.S. partners have the AP to their safeguards agreement with the IAEA in effect. The exceptions are Argentina, Brazil, and Egypt, which have neither signed nor ratified the AP. India and Thailand have signed but not ratified the AP as of August 2012. With the entry into force of the AP to the U.S. voluntary safeguards agreement with the IAEA in 2009, the United States is now in a more credible position to insist on the AP in new agreements. Two countries considering peaceful nuclear cooperation agreements with the United States—Malaysia and Vietnam—do not have Additional Protocols in effect.

TREATIES AND INTERNATIONAL AGREEMENTS

Treaty on the Non-Proliferation of Nuclear Weapons. The NPT Review Conference of 2010 was unable to reach agreement for supporting a proposal by the United States and several other states to make the AP "the IAEA safeguards standard." The members of the Non-Aligned Movement opposed this proposal and stressed the voluntary nature of the AP. The final document, however, did note that in the case of a state party with a comprehensive safeguards agreement supplemented by an AP in force, measures contained in both instruments represent "the enhanced safeguards standard."

Nuclear Suppliers Group. The NSG has thus far been unable to reach a consensus on requiring the AP as a condition of supply for Trigger-List items, since some members insist that it is a voluntary measure and not required by the NPT. However, the NSG does require the AP as a condition of supply for enrichment and reprocessing equipment and technology, but with an important exception.[35] One member of the NSG—Australia—

34. Among other things, the AP gives the agency the right to increased information and access to all aspects of a state's nuclear fuel cycle—from uranium mines to nuclear wastes and to locations where nuclear material intended for nonnuclear uses is intended. It gives complementary access rights to its inspectors, e.g., access is possible to any place on a "site" or to mines or to nuclear-related locations where no nuclear material is located, such as sites where related research and development or manufacturing activities are performed, to ensure the absence of undeclared activities. The AP also permits environmental sampling on the basis of either location-specific, or under certain conditions, wide-area monitoring.

35. Paragraph (c) of the guidelines provide that pending the entry into force of an Additional Protocol, suppliers may authorize transfers only when the recipient "is implementing appropriate safeguards agreements in cooperation with the IAEA, including a regional accounting and control arrangement for nuclear materials, as approved by the IAEA Board of Governors." This loophole covers Argentina and Brazil by virtue of the Quadrilateral Safeguards Agreement and bilateral accounting agency, as mentioned above. However, it should be noted that the authorities of the ABACC and that safeguards agreement are by no

now requires an Additional Protocol to be in force for any country importing uranium from Australia.[36]

UN Security Council Resolution 1887. Resolution 1887 calls on all states to sign, ratify, and implement an Additional Protocol, which together with comprehensive safeguards agreements, constitutes essential elements of the IAEA safeguards system. It also encourages states to consider whether a recipient state has signed and ratified an Additional Protocol based on the Model AP in making nuclear export decisions.

Report of the Commission of Eminent Persons on the Future of the IAEA. The report has also recommended that "supplier states should make the Additional Protocol a condition for granting export licenses of nuclear materials, services, and technologies."

> *The IAEA reports that as of October 23, 2012, 119 states plus EURATOM and Taiwan have an AP in force. Thus, notwithstanding the reservations of some states about making the AP a condition of supply or the IAEA safeguards standard, the AP has gained wide acceptance as an international norm. However, there remain some important holdouts such as Argentina and Brazil.*

Fall-Back Safeguards

So-called fall-back safeguards are a means of ensuring the continuity of safeguards, if the IAEA is not applying or cannot apply safeguards in a country or if a state withdraws from the NPT and renounces its NPT safeguards agreement. A requirement for fall-back safeguards would allow the supplier government to insist that some other form of safeguards be applied to the nuclear material subject to the agreement with the withdrawing state. The fall-back safeguards policy reinforces the principle of perpetuity of safeguards and helps mitigate the weakness in the NPT that allows a state that withdraws from the treaty to renounce its NPT safeguards agreement.

UNITED STATES. The United States, as a matter of policy, includes provisions in its post-NNPA agreements for peaceful nuclear cooperation that, in the event that the IAEA cannot or is not

---

means equivalent to the authorities of the IAEA under the Additional Protocol, which is precisely the reason Argentina and Brazil object to the AP—it would give more authority to the IAEA than to its own inspectors.

36. "Australia's Network of Nuclear Safeguards Agreements," Australian Department of Foreign Affairs and Trade, http://www.dfat.gov.au/security/nuclear_safeguards.html.

applying safeguards, the United States has the right to apply bilateral safeguards.[37] Such fall-back safeguards have never been applied.

TREATIES AND INTERNATIONAL AGREEMENTS

Treaty on the Non-Proliferation of Nuclear Weapons. The NPT itself does not have a provision for the continuation of safeguards in the event that a country withdraws from the treaty, as evidenced by the termination of North Korea's safeguards agreement with the IAEA after it withdrew from the NPT in 2002.

Nuclear Suppliers Group. The NSG guidelines provide (para.4 9a) that "if the IAEA decides that the application of IAEA safeguards is no longer possible, the supplier and recipient should elaborate appropriate verification measures. If the recipient does not accept these measures, it should allow at the request of the supplier the restitution of transferred and derived Trigger-List items." However, this guideline does not apply to agreements or contracts drawn up on or before April 3, 1992.

The U.S. policy on fall-back safeguards is contained in all nuclear cooperation agreements after 1978. The NSG guideline applies only to prospective supply commitments entered into after April 3, 1992. No state has implemented any fall-back safeguards to date, but they remain an important instrument in ensuring the perpetuity of verification of supplied materials in the event that the IAEA cannot apply safeguards or if a state withdraws from the NPT.

Safeguards in Nuclear-Weapon States

United States. U.S. law does not require safeguards on nuclear exports to nuclear-weapon states.[38] In its agreement with EURATOM, U.S. nuclear exports to the United Kingdom and France are subject to EURATOM safeguards. In addition, materials subject to the U.S.-EURATOM agreement

37. In addition, the U.S.-EURATOM agreement provides that, in the event that the IAEA is not applying safeguards in accordance with the safeguards agreements noted above, the European Union shall enter into an agreement or agreements with the IAEA that provide for effectiveness and coverage equivalent to that provided by the safeguards agreements they are replacing. If that is not possible, the European Community shall give the United States an assurance that it will apply safeguards itself that are equivalent in effectiveness and coverage to the IAEA safeguards they are replacing. Only in the event that both the IAEA and the European Community are not applying safeguards does the U.S.-EURATOM Agreement provide for the application of safeguards by the United States. In this case the agreement states that the parties shall immediately establish safeguards arrangements equivalent in effectiveness and scope to the IAEA safeguards they are replacing.

38. Nuclear-weapon states are defined by the NPT as those states having manufactured and detonated a nuclear weapons or other nuclear explosive device before January 1, 1967—China, the United States, Russia, the United Kingdom, and France. Other states that possess or have tested a nuclear weapon or nuclear explosive device—India, Israel, Pakistan, and North Korea—are not recognized as nuclear-weapon states by the NPT.

are subject to the voluntary safeguards agreements that France and the United Kingdom have concluded with the IAEA. In turn, items exported from EURATOM to the United States under the U.S.-EURATOM agreement are subject to the U.S. voluntary safeguards agreement with the IAEA. The U.S. agreement with the Russian Federation includes a reciprocal requirement for submitting nuclear items subject to the agreement to the two countries' respective voluntary safeguards agreements with the IAEA. India is not recognized as a nuclear-weapon state by the NPT, but the U.S. agreement with India requires India to enter into a safeguards agreement with the IAEA that covers facilities that New Delhi identified as part of its peaceful nuclear program. In its agreement with China, the United States has rights to information and to visits to material, equipment, and components subject to the agreement in lieu of safeguards.

TREATIES AND INTERNATIONAL AGREEMENTS

Treaty on the Non-Proliferation of Nuclear Weapons. Nuclear-weapon states party to the NPT are not obligated to subject their nuclear activities to IAEA safeguards. However, the five nuclear-weapon states that are party to the treaty have entered into so-called voluntary safeguards agreements with the IAEA. The voluntary safeguards agreements of nuclear-weapon states party to the NPT have important limitations. With a few exceptions, the IAEA does not actually apply safeguards in the nuclear-weapon states due to a lack of financial resources. In addition, the voluntary safeguards agreements of the United States, Russia, and China with the agency allow each of those states to withdraw nuclear materials or facilities eligible for the application of IAEA safeguards. All peaceful nuclear activities in the United States are eligible for IAEA safeguards application. Russia and China have submitted only a few facilities to their voluntary safeguards agreements with the IAEA. The 2000 NPT Review Conference called for the wider application of safeguards to peaceful nuclear facilities in the nuclear-weapon states under the relevant voluntary-offer safeguards agreements in the most economical and practical way possible, taking into account the availability of IAEA resources. However, the nuclear-weapon states have not moved to implement this recommendation.

EURATOM Treaty. Under the EURATOM Treaty, France and the United Kingdom have placed all their peaceful nuclear activities under EURATOM safeguards.

Zangger Committee and Nuclear Suppliers Group. The guidelines of these multilateral export regimes do not contain any provision calling for safeguards on nuclear exports to nuclear-weapon states.

OTHER COUNTRIES

India has entered into a voluntary safeguards agreement with the IAEA as a condition of its concluding a peaceful nuclear cooperation agreement with the United States that covers those facilities that India has declared as civil. However, India's voluntary safeguards agreement with the IAEA does not allow it to withdraw materials or facilities from safeguards since it is an IAEA INFCIRC/66/Rev. 2 safeguards agreement.

Although nuclear-weapon states are not obligated to accept safeguards on their nuclear activities, all the NPT nuclear-weapon states have entered into voluntary safeguards agreements with the IAEA in which they designate facilities as eligible for safeguards. France and the United Kingdom place all their peaceful nuclear activities under EURATOM safeguards. In some cases, suppliers have required specific safeguards requirements in their nuclear cooperation agreements with nuclear-weapon states. For example, Japan required China to accept IAEA safeguards on its supplies to the Qinshan nuclear power reactor, and Russia requires IAEA safeguards in connection with its export of centrifuge technology to China. The Shaanzi enrichment plant is under IAEA safeguards, and the enrichment plant at Lanzhou is eligible for safeguards, but the IAEA has not chosen to implement safeguards there.

Physical Protection

HEU awaiting secure transportation by rail. Credit: NNSA 2010. http://www.flickr.com/photos/nnsanews/5074622925/.

Requiring a guarantee that supplier materials and equipment will be subject to internationally accepted physical protection measures is necessary to preventing or deterring non-state actors such as terrorists or criminal organizations from obtaining nuclear-weapons-usable materials or from sabotaging nuclear facilities.

UNITED STATES. The AEA, section 123 (a) (6), requires a guarantee that adequate physical protection be maintained with respect to items subject to the agreement. While the formulation differs from agreement to agreement, the United States typically requires that cooperating partners establish physical protection measures that meet the criteria set out in the Convention on the Physical Protection of Nuclear Material and the NSG guidelines (which are identical), taking into account the recommendations of the IAEA in INFCIRC/225/Rev.5 or in any revision or replacement of that document. Recent U.S. agreements with Australia and Russia go further in providing that, in addition to its obligations under the CPPNM, "each Party shall apply measures of physical protection in accordance with its national legislation which meet levels not less than the recommendations of Agency document INFCIRC/225/Rev.4 (corrected) or in any revision or replacement of that document." However, this requirement has not been standard in U.S. agreements. The U.S. agreement with Egypt provides that the United States will assist Egypt in establishing mutually agreed physical protection arrangements to be applied by the government of Egypt. The U.S.-UAE agreement goes even further and provides that the United States and the UAE shall cooperate in establishing mutually agreed physical protection measures to be applied by the UAE and that both the CPPNM and the IAEA recommendations will be taken into account in assessing whether the UAE is fulfilling its physical protection obligations under the agreement. In addition, the United States has had the practice of conducting physical protection visits to and exchanging information on best practices with states that possess weapons-usable materials of U.S. origin. U.S. efforts to promote physical protection internationally have been hampered by the fact that the U.S. Congress, at this writing, has not enacted the legislation necessary to implement the amended CPPNM.

TREATIES AND INTERNATIONAL AGREEMENTS

Convention on the Physical Protection of Nuclear Materials. The CPPNM is the only international legally binding agreement for the physical protection of nuclear material. It establishes measures related to the prevention, detection, and punishment of offenses relating to nuclear material. The convention originally applied only to nuclear material used for peaceful purposes while in international transport and did not cover nuclear materials in domestic use. States took the position that physical protection is a national responsibility and therefore not subject to binding international standards. It took the 9/11 terrorist attacks to persuade most states that the CPPNM should provide for protection of nuclear materials within their territories. Parties to the CPPNM then adopted an amendment to expand the convention's scope to cover the physical protection of nuclear material in domestic use, storage, and transport and the protection of nuclear materials and facilities against sabotage. It also provides for expanded cooperation between and among states on rapid measures to locate and recover stolen or smuggled nuclear material, mitigate any radiological consequences of sabotage, and prevent and combat related offences. The amendment has not yet entered into force.

The CPPNM prescribes only very general levels of physical protections, which are the same as those required of cooperating partners in most U.S. agreements for cooperation and with those set out in the NSG guidelines, and does not provide high security standards, leaving much to the discretion of each national government in applying specific measures.

UN Security Council Resolution 1540. In 2004, the UN Security Council adopted Resolution 1540, which set a new global requirement for all countries to "develop and maintain appropriate effective physical protection measures" to protect their nuclear material and facilities. However, it did not prescribe the characteristics of the measures the states were to adopt, nor did it define what it meant by *appropriate* or *effective*. The resolution created a committee to interpret and implement Resolution 1540. This committee's role so far has been to urge states to supply the reports on what they have done to implement the resolution, to review those reports, and to call on those states that have not answered questions adequately or have not yet submitted a report to do so.

IAEA Physical Protection Recommendations. In 1972, the International Atomic Energy Agency published "Recommendations for the Physical Protection of Nuclear Material," which were prepared by a panel of experts convened by the director general. INFCIRC/225 does not impose legal obligations on states and leaves it to each individual state whether and how it implements the physical protection recommendations set forth in the IAEA document. However, INFCIRC/225 does reflect a broad international consensus on the requirements for the physical protection of nuclear material and facilities and provides specific guidance for states in establishing and implementing their physical protection systems. From time to time, INFCIRC/225 has been revised. Recent changes have included specific recommendations related to sabotage of nuclear facilities and nuclear material. As a result, the title of the document was changed to "The Physical Protection of Nuclear Material and Nuclear Facilities." The newest revision (rev. 5) includes guidance on the rapid recovery of missing nuclear material and the mitigation of sabotage. It also introduces the concept of a physical protection "regime" and strengthens performance testing to include force-on-force exercises as well as a graded approach to physical protection that takes into account the threat, the relative attractiveness of the material, and the potential consequences associated with theft or sabotage. Finally, INFCIRC/225/Revision 5 provides clearer physical protection guidance for states that may be developing peaceful nuclear energy for the first time.

Nuclear Suppliers Group. The NSG guidelines require physical protection as a condition of nuclear exports and refer to the same general levels of physical protection as contained in the CPPNM that should be met for different categories of nuclear materials. They note, paragraph 3(b), that implementation of measures of physical protection in the recipient country is the responsibility of the government of that country but that the levels of physical protection should be the subject of an agreement between supplier and recipient. The guidelines also note that INFCIRC/225 and similar documents are a useful basis for guiding recipient states in designing a system of physical protection measures and procedures. In addition, the NSG guidelines state that "suppliers should promote international co-operation in the areas of physical security through the exchange of physical security information, protection of nuclear materials in transit, and recovery of stolen nuclear materials and equipment. Suppliers should promote broadest adherence to the respective international instruments, inter alia, to the Convention on the Physical Protection of Nuclear Material, as well as implementation of INFCIRC/225, as amended from time to time."

The Nuclear Security Summits held in Washington in 2010 and in Seoul in 2012 raised global awareness of the threat of nuclear terrorism and encouraged states to improve the security of nuclear materials and facilities. Among other things, they encouraged universal adherence to CPPNM and set a target date of 2014 for its entry into force. Although considerable work needs to be done, the critical importance of protecting nuclear materials and facilities is increasingly recognized.

The criteria for physical protection that are set out in an annex to U.S. agreements are the same as those found in the NSG guidelines and the CPPNM. However, these criteria fall far short of what is necessary to provide adequate protection for nuclear materials and facilities. They describe only very general levels of physical protection and establish no specific standards or measures for protecting nuclear materials. Physical protection is universally regarded as the sovereign responsibility of the country that possesses the materials, and therefore there is strong resistance to a standardized set of physical protection measures. The IAEA recommendations on physical protection set out far more detailed measures for securing nuclear materials and facilities. While the NSG guidelines take note of the IAEA recommendations, they do not require them as a condition of supply.

Transfers of Sensitive Nuclear Technology

IAEA safeguards inspectors together with the experts from the Czech State Office for Nuclear Safety jointly verify a load of high-enriched uranium fuel held in special Skoda casks before it is brought back to Russia. Credit: Dean Calma/IAEA 2007. http://www.iaea.org/NewsCenter/Multimedia/Imagebank/index.jsp/.

Suppliers exercise special restraint and controls on the transfer of enrichment and reprocessing technology and equipment because such technologies can produce materials that can be directly used in a nuclear weapon. Several aspects of enrichment technologies remain classified as restricted data, while reprocessing technology has been declassified for many years.[39]

UNITED STATES. The AEA, section 123 (a) (9), requires a guarantee that special nuclear material and any facilities produced or constructed by or through the use of sensitive nuclear technology (enrichment, reprocessing, and heavy water technology) transferred pursuant to an agreement be subject to all the nonproliferation requirements set out in section 123 of the AEA. However, most U.S. agreements for peaceful nuclear cooperation prohibit the transfer of sensi-

39. Section 4 (5) of the Nuclear Non-Proliferation Act of 1978 defines sensitive nuclear technology as "technology not available to the public which is important to the design, construction, fabrication, operation or maintenance of an enrichment, reprocessing or heavy water production facility." (This is similar to the definition of sensitive nuclear technology found in the Nuclear Suppliers Guidelines.) Section 57 (b) of the AEA allows the export of such technology either pursuant to an agreement for cooperation or "upon authorization by the secretary of energy after a determination that such activity will not be inimical to the interest of the United States."

Section 11.y of the AEA defines restricted data as meaning "all data concerning (1) design, manufacture, or utilization of atomic weapons; (2) the production of special nuclear material; or (3) the use of special nuclear material in the production of energy, but shall not include data declassified or removed from the Restricted Data category pursuant to section 142." Section 144 of the AEA stipulates that restricted data may be transferred to another nation for peaceful purposes only pursuant to a peaceful nuclear cooperation agreement in accordance with section 123 of the AEA.

tive nuclear technology and restricted data under the agreement or require an amendment to the agreement for such transfer.[40]

Sensitive nuclear technology as well as other nuclear technology may be transferred outside an agreement. Section 57 (b) of the AEA governs the export of technology, providing that

> it shall be unlawful for any person to directly or indirectly engage in the production of any special nuclear material outside of the United States except (1) as specifically authorized under an agreement for cooperation made pursuant to section 123, including a specific authorization in a subsequent arrangement under section 131 of this Act, or (2) upon authorization by the Secretary of Energy after a determination that such activity will not be inimical to the interest of the United States….

The 10 Code of Federal Regulations Part 810, which implements section 57 (b) of the AEA, states that an export of nuclear technology does not require a specific authorization of the secretary of energy when the information is already in the public domain, when it is for radiological emergencies, or when it is given in connection with IAEA programs or involves assistance to civilian nuclear power in countries that share U.S. nonproliferation objectives. However, certain kinds of assistance do require the secretary's specific authorization:

- Assistance to civilian nuclear power in countries on the list contained in section 810.8 of the Code of Federal Regulations. (U.S. assistance to countries on the 810.8 list would be granted only after careful interagency review and under conditions ensuring no use for nuclear explosives or in unsafeguarded fuel-cycle activities.)
- Assistance to enrichment, reprocessing, plutonium fuel fabrication, heavy water production, or research and to test reactors above five megawatts thermal in any country.

The Department of Energy is now proposing to make revisions to 10 Code for Federal Regulations Part 810 that, among other things, would allow the transfer of generally authorized activities only to states that have agreements for cooperation with the United States.

With the exception of a special U.S. agreement with Australia that provides for the transfer of Silex enrichment technology, the United States does not export sensitive nuclear technology.[41]

Moreover, U.S. laws impose sanctions on the transfer of sensitive nuclear technology by other suppliers. U.S. foreign assistance law provides for the cutoff of economic and military assistance to countries that transfer or receive enrichment or reprocessing technology, and the AEA provides for the termination of nuclear cooperation with any countries that enter into an agreement for the transfer of enrichment or reprocessing materials and equipment.[42]

---

40. An exception to this policy is the U.S.-Canada agreement on peaceful nuclear cooperation. While that agreement allows for the transfers of sensitive nuclear technology, no such transfer has taken place since the entry into force of the latest amendment to that agreement in 1980. In addition, the United States and Australia have concluded an agreement providing for cooperation in developing laser enrichment technology.

41. In the late 1980s, the U.S. Department of Energy transferred breeder reactor reprocessing technology to Japan but determined that this was not sensitive nuclear technology since Japan already possessed such technology.

42. The Symington and the Glenn amendments to the Foreign Assistance Act provide for the cutoff of military and economic assistance to countries importing or exporting enrichment and reprocessing tech-

TREATIES AND INTERNATIONAL AGREEMENTS

Nuclear Suppliers Group. The original NSG guidelines called for the exercise of restraint in the export of sensitive nuclear technology and weapons-usable materials and recommended supplier involvement or multinational management of such facilities as an alternative to national plants. In his speech on February 11, 2004, President George W. Bush made a proposal that went well beyond that guideline by suggesting that NSG members refuse to sell such technology to any state that does not already possess full-scale and functioning enrichment and reprocessing plants. Members of the NSG rejected this proposal in favor of a new criteria-based approach. In June 2011, the NSG adopted a revised guideline (paragraphs 6 and 7) establishing agreed criteria that limit the transfer of enrichment and reprocessing technologies only to a state that is in compliance with its nonproliferation objectives, is an NPT party, and meets agreed standards of safeguards, physical protection, and safety. The criteria also call for suppliers to transfer enrichment technologies, equipment, or entire facilities only under "black-box conditions." This means the supply of such items only under conditions that do not permit or enable replication of the facilities.

In addition to these guidelines on the transfer of sensitive nuclear technology, in 1995 the members of the NSG agreed that the fundamental principles for safeguards and export controls of the guidelines set out in INFCIRC/254/Part 1 should apply to technology directly associated with any Trigger-List items. As a result, the nonexplosive use, comprehensive safeguards, retransfer, and other provisions of the guidelines were applied to all nuclear-related technology transfers as well as to materials, equipment, and components.

UN Security Council Resolution 1887. Resolution 1887 calls on states to adopt stricter national controls for the export of sensitive goods and technologies of the nuclear fuel cycle.

U.S. law and policy and the NSG guidelines on nuclear technology exports go beyond the ZC and the NPT. The NPT does not control nuclear technology since article III.2 of the NPT applies to the export of source or special fissionable material or equipment or material especially designed or prepared for the processing, use, or production of special fissionable material. It does not apply to information on the design of such facilities.

---

nology, respectively. Both of these amendments allow that the president to waive the sanctions if he can determine that certain very difficult waiver standards are met. Faced with clear evidence of transfers of enrichment technology to Pakistan and an inability to satisfy the applicable waiver standard of the Symington amendment, President Carter halted economic and security assistance to Pakistan in April 1979. The same year, however, the Soviets invaded Afghanistan and thus put Pakistan in the forefront of efforts to counter Soviet efforts to upset the balance of power in South Asia. President Carter offered Pakistan $400 million in military aid, but President Zia spurned this offer as "peanuts." After President Reagan came into power, Congress in 1981 authorized the president to put aside the Symington amendment prohibitions on economic and military assistance to Pakistan until 1987 under a special waiver authority.

In practice, major nuclear suppliers have limited their transfers of enrichment and reprocessing technology to states that already possess enrichment and reprocessing capabilities and these have been rare, open, and legal transfers. One exception was proposed Russian assistance to the Iranian nuclear program. In 1995, the United States became aware that, in addition to signing an agreement to complete the Bushehr reactor in Iran, the Russians had agreed in a secret protocol to provide the Iranians with key fuel-cycle facilities, including a uranium enrichment centrifuge plant. The United States immediately pressed the Russians to terminate all assistance to the Iranian nuclear program. While Russia did not cancel its lucrative Bushehr reactor deal, it did limit its nuclear cooperation with Iran to the reactor project. Notwithstanding this commitment, Russian entities engaged in extensive cooperation with Iranian nuclear research centers, which was outside the bounds of the Bushehr project.

Other than the Russian transfer to Iran, most transfers have been of enrichment technology under black-box conditions to the United States. The Enrichment Technology Corporation, an entity established by the Uranium Enrichment Corporation, or URENCO, that actually holds centrifuge technology, has allowed the French firm AREVA to build an enrichment plant at Eagle Rock, Idaho, in the United States, under black-box conditions. Also, URENCO governments (the United Kingdom, the Netherlands, and Germany) have transferred centrifuge technology to URENCO USA, both under black-box conditions for the URENCO USA facility in New Mexico. Russia also has made centrifuge technology available to China under black-box conditions.[43]

The major problem with transfers of sensitive nuclear technologies has not been exports by the major nuclear suppliers but clandestine and illicit supplies of such technologies outside of the NSG by states such as Pakistan and North Korea. The potential for such transfers remains a matter of serious concern that could present a major threat to the nonproliferation regime.

Requiring special controls on transfers of enrichment and reprocessing technology and equipment has become standard practice among major nuclear suppliers. However, the idea of restricting the transfer of sensitive enrichment and reprocessing technologies is far from a universally accepted international norm, as proposals to limit the spread of these technologies have been the subject of heated debate within the NSG, the IAEA Board of Governors, and the NPT Review Conference and in bilateral negotiations that the United States has conducted with individual states. Many non-nuclear-weapon states insist that they have rights under the NPT to possess such facilities and have made clear that they do not intend to foreclose the opportunity to acquire such technology or to forgo their rights to do so.

43. Australia has transferred Silex technology to the United States but not under black-box conditions.

Exports of Weapons-Usable Materials

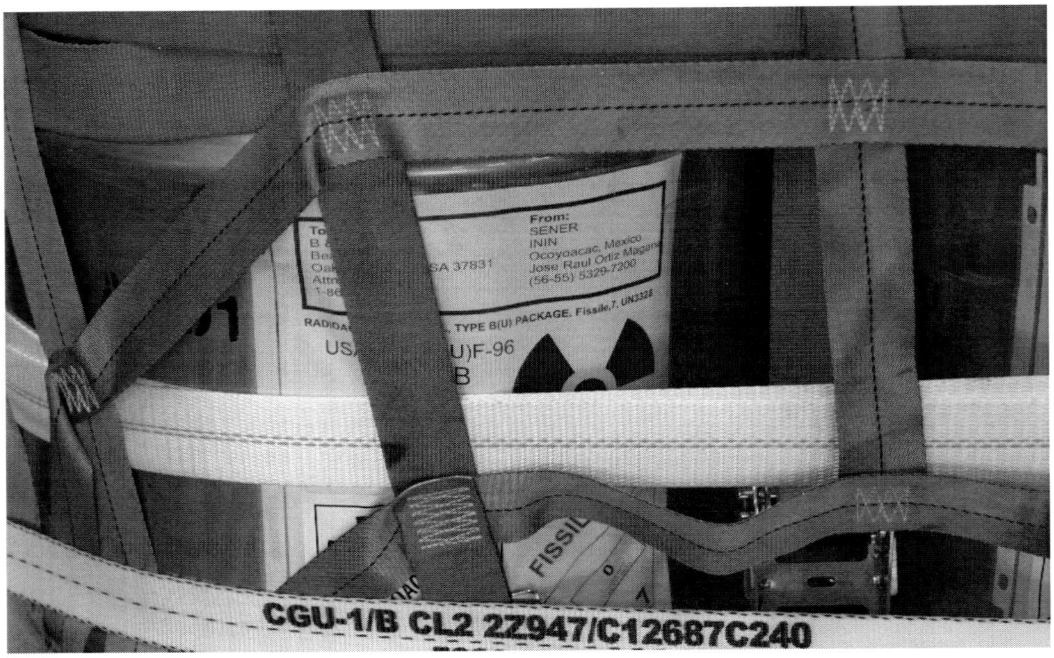

Casks of high-enriched uranium. Credit: NNSA 2012. http://www.flickr.com/photos/nnsanews/7017089541/.

The export of weapons-usable materials—highly enriched uranium or separated plutonium—is no longer widely accepted as it was many years ago, but policies are not consistent across the board.

UNITED STATES. As a matter of policy, the United States does not export plutonium for peaceful purposes. However, as will be discussed below, the United States has consented to the use and transfers of plutonium in EURATOM and Japan.

In the past, the United States exported HEU to fuel research reactors and fast-neutron reactors, space propulsion, and medical isotope production. In the late 1970s, in efforts to reduce the threat of the misuse of HEU in civilian applications, the United States focused on developing replacement fuels, converting HEU-fueled research reactors to use low-enriched uranium, and repatriating HEU spent fuel from foreign countries. In 1992, the United States enacted the "Schumer amendment" to the Energy Policy Act, which required foreign reactors supplied with HEU fuel by the United States to commit to converting to LEU as quickly as possible and prohibited exports of HEU to foreign reactors, if they did not undertake such obligations. The implementation of this amendment, in combination with LEU fuel development and a drop in the construction of new reactors, facilitated a rapid decline in U.S. HEU exports. On July 29, 2005, Congress passed the Energy Policy Act of 2005, which included provisions relaxing restrictions on HEU exports for medical isotope production. The new law permits the export of U.S. HEU to medical isotope producers even if they refuse to convert to LEU. In recent years, there have been only a handful of HEU exports for that purpose. In 2012, the United States announced a number of measures to encourage reliable supplies of molybdenum-99 (MO-99) produced without highly enriched uranium, including steps to further reduce exports of HEU for medical isotope production when sufficient supplies of non-HEU-produced MO-99 are available to the global marketplace.

TREATIES AND INTERNATIONAL AGREEMENTS

Nuclear Suppliers Group. The NSG calls for restraint in the export of weapons-usable materials but imposes no explicit ban on exports of plutonium or HEU for civilian purposes, provided recipients meet the NSG guidelines. Other suppliers do not impose restrictions on HEU exports such as those required by U.S. law. As a result, some countries have imported HEU supplies from other countries rather than from the United States. Russia, for example, concluded agreements to supply HEU for research reactors in Canada and in some countries in the European Union (for reactors in France, Germany, and the Netherlands).[44]

Plutonium Guidelines. "Guidelines on the Management of Plutonium" (INFCIRC/549)—adopted by Belgium, China, France, Germany, Japan, the Russian Federation, Switzerland, the United Kingdom, and the United States in 1998—stipulate that plutonium will not be further transferred to a third country without the prior consent of the government of the original supplier. Moreover, the intended recipient must provide a certificate stating the quantity, the approximate date of delivery, the final destination and end-use, and the timetable for use before transferring separated plutonium exceeding 50 grams to a recipient country in any 12-month period. These guidelines also provide that any proposed shipment of separated plutonium be discussed between the supplying and the recipient governments in light of their nonproliferation commitments, the information published by the recipient government on its holdings of separated plutonium and its strategy for plutonium use, the intended recipient's certificate of end-use, and other relevant circumstances.

Other Countries. The Declaration of Common Policy in the European Union allows for the transfer of plutonium and HEU among member states only on receipt of a certificate from the consignee specifying the final destination, the quantities, the approximate date of delivery, the timetable for use, the form in which delivery is to take place, and the allocation of the material to specified peaceful uses. It also prohibits plutonium and HEU from being retransferred to a third state without mutual agreement between the member state that has separated the plutonium or enriched the uranium to more than 20 percent and the member state desiring to effect the retransfer, without prejudice to any other rights of prior consent that may exist. The prior agreement of the supplying state will be required for any retransfer of installations, principal components of crucial importance, reprocessing or enrichment technology, or the technology of heavy water production, as well as for any transfer of installations or principal components of crucial importance derived therefrom. Such retransfers and transfers between member states may take place in consultation with the originating member state in light of the nature and the degree of development of the nuclear program of the receiving member state.

44. "Past and Current Civilian HEU Reduction Efforts," Nuclear Threat Initiative, July 25, 2011, http://www.nti.org/analysis/articles/past-and-current-civilian-heu-reduction-efforts/.

Suppliers have generally exercised restraint in the export of weapons-usable nuclear material. The market for plutonium is limited to a few countries, and the demand for HEU is confined to use in a few research reactors for either various research purposes or medical isotope production. The development of new technologies that do not rely on HEU could potentially increase the prospects for eliminating HEU from international nuclear commerce.

Prior Consent Rights

The interim storage pool at the UP-3 reprocessing plant in La Hague. Photo courtesy of IAEA. Credit: Areva (Cogema) 1992. http://www.iaea.org/NewsCenter/Multimedia/Imagebank/index.jsp.

Supplier "consent rights" require that a cooperating partner obtain the prior approval of the supplier government before undertaking certain activities with respect to the nuclear materials it receives under a nuclear cooperation agreement. Consent rights can apply to retransfers of nuclear materials and equipment to third countries, the enrichment of uranium and the reprocessing or alteration of spent fuel produced from such materials, and the use or storage of plutonium, HEU, or uranium-233. Suppliers require their approval of these operations because they recognize them as sensitive nuclear activities that can involve or produce materials that can be used directly in a nuclear weapon.

Retransfers

Nuclear export controls would have little meaning if recipients were able to retransfer supplied nuclear material, equipment, or components or special nuclear material produced through their use to a third country without the same or comparable nonproliferation conditions. Hence, supplier consent rights on retransfers are essential to preserving controls on directly transferred materials and equipment.

UNITED STATES. U.S. law, AEA section 123 (a) (5), requires a U.S. right of prior consent for retransfers of nuclear material and equipment subject to a U.S. agreement for peaceful nuclear cooperation. In other words, the United States must approve transfers before they happen and has the right to veto such transfers. Implementing retransfer consent rights has varied from country to country, however. The United States has consented to retransfers on a shipment-by-shipment basis and on an "advance consent" basis.

> ***Shipment-by-Shipment Retransfer Consent.*** In the 1970s, the United States granted consent on a shipment-by-shipment basis for such countries as Japan, Spain, Sweden, and Switzerland to transfer their U.S.-obligated spent fuel to EURATOM for reprocessing. However, the United States retained prior consent rights on the further disposition of the recovered plutonium.[45]
>
> ***Advance Retransfer Consent.*** The United States has given a one-time advance consent to Japan to retransfer unirradiated natural uranium and low-enriched uranium to countries with which the United States has an agreement for cooperation but not for the production of highly enriched uranium. This means that Japan can retransfer such material without prior U.S. approval (but must notify the United States of the transfer). Similarly, the United States has given advance consent to EURATOM to transfer low-enriched uranium, natural uranium, and nuclear equipment to countries with which the United States has peaceful nuclear cooperation agreements for use in their programs but not for reprocessing or enrichment above 20 percent. The United States has also given advance consent to Japan and Switzerland to retransfer U.S.-obligated spent fuel to EURATOM for reprocessing and fabrication of mixed-oxide fuel (MOX) fuel elements and for the return of MOX fuel elements from EURATOM to Japan and Switzerland for use in specified facilities as part of their plutonium recycling programs.[46] In each case, the retransferred materials remain subject to the terms and conditions of the U.S. agreement with those countries.
>
> In its agreements with Norway and the UAE, the United States granted advance consent to transfer spent fuel from these states to EURATOM for reprocessing. Under these consent arrangements, Norway and the UAE may not transfer any plutonium recovered from such reprocessing without the further consent of the United States. In both the Norwegian and the UAE cases, any U.S.-obligated spent fuel these countries would transfer to EURATOM would be subject to the terms and conditions of the U.S.-EURATOM agreement.
>
> The agreements described above are not the norm for the U.S. approach to exercising its retransfer consent rights. Most other U.S. cooperating partners have not requested or been granted advance U.S. consent to retransfer items subject to their agreements with the United States. In cases where the United States has given advance consent to retransfers

45. The United States maintained control over plutonium because it is a material that is directly usable in nuclear weapons. Thus the plutonium had to remain stored at the reprocessing facilities in EURATOM until the United States consented to its use.

46. U.S. consent does not include approval of reprocessing of U.S.-obligated spent fuel in Switzerland, only the use of recovered plutonium in Swiss civil nuclear reactors.

for reprocessing, they involved close allies with advanced nuclear programs and strong nonproliferation credentials. In the case of the UAE, advance retransfer consent was meant to create a potential option for the UAE in the future to send its spent fuel abroad for reprocessing.

TREATIES AND INTERNATIONAL AGREEMENTS

The NSG guidelines call for a right of prior approval for retransfer as a condition of exporting Trigger-List items. For most nuclear items and related technology, paragraph 9 (a) of the NSG guidelines requires the recipient to extend assurances from the original transfer to subsequent transfers. This requirement applies both to the retransfer of such items or related technology and to the transfer of Trigger-List items derived from facilities originally transferred by the supplier or with the help of equipment or technology originally transferred by the supplier. A few suppliers such as Japan and South Korea require, as does the United States, a specific consent to retransfer.

In addition, the NSG guidelines call for specific government-to-government assurance for retransfer of (1) any Trigger-List items or related technology from any state whose export policy does not require comprehensive safeguards as a condition of supply; (2) enrichment, reprocessing, or heavy water production facilities, equipment, or related technology; (3) facilities or equipment of the same type derived from items originally transferred by the supplier; and (4) heavy water or material usable for nuclear weapons or other nuclear explosive devices.

OTHER COUNTRIES

Both Australia and Canada have given the United States consent to retransfer materials they export to the United States to EURATOM and Japan for use in their respective peaceful nuclear programs on a long-term basis. Australia has given Russia long-term consent to transfer Australian-obligated nuclear materials to third countries with which Australia has an agreement for purposes of conversion, enrichment below 20 percent in the isotope uranium-235, fuel fabrication, or use in a reactor.

The United States has granted advance consent for retransfers of spent fuel to EURATOM for reprocessing and the return of the recovered plutonium to Japan and Switzerland for use in civil nuclear reactors. For some countries, the United States provided consent on a shipment-by-shipment basis for the retransfer of spent fuel to EURATOM for reprocessing.

The retransfer consent right found in most U.S. agreements is broader than that found in the NSG guidelines, since specific U.S. consent must be obtained for retransfer of any material or item subject to the U.S. agreement. As a minimum requirement, the recipient country must have a peaceful nuclear cooperation agreement with the United States.

> *For retransfers of most Trigger-List items, the NSG guidelines require the recipient of the retransfer to provide the same assurances as those required by the supplier for the original transfer. This requirement amounts to an advance consent to retransfer most Trigger-List items to any country that accepts the relevant NSG conditions. However, the main holders of plutonium have agreed on more rigorous requirements for the transfer of this weapons-usable material.*
>
> *The consent that major suppliers have thus far granted to retransfer spent fuel for reprocessing or for the use of plutonium has not been widespread and has been limited to a few advanced nuclear states in Western Europe and Japan.*

Consent to Enrichment

Enrichment plants can enrich natural uranium to fuel-grade material (3–5 percent U-235), but the same technology can enrich uranium to weapons grade (normally 90–95 percent U-235). Hence, suppliers will often require consent to enrich the uranium they supply to prevent the production of HEU.

UNITED STATES. Section 123 (a) (7) of the AEA requires a guarantee by the cooperating party that no U.S.-obligated nuclear material may be enriched without the prior approval of the United States.[47] Some U.S. agreements give consent to enrichment up to less than 20 percent, while others require consent for any enrichment.

TREATIES AND INTERNATIONAL AGREEMENTS

The NSG guidelines have no provision for consent to enrichment of supplied nuclear materials. Australia and Canada require consent for enrichment above 20 percent. Japan has reciprocal consent rights on enrichment (beyond 20 percent) in its agreements with the United States, Australia, Canada, and South Korea. In its agreement with Russia, Japan has consent rights over enrichment. Japan's agreements with Jordan and Vietnam prohibit them from enriching nuclear material subject to their individual agreements with Japan.

A number of countries that do not participate in the NSG are suppliers of uranium to the international market. Major producers of uranium such as Niger, Namibia, and Uzbekistan do not require consent rights over enrichment reprocessing and other activities.[48] Although they are parties to the NPT, the treaty does not obligate suppliers to have consent rights for sensitive operations on their natural uranium exports. However, if these uranium producers export nuclear material to NSG participants—for example, for conversion, enrichment, or fuel fabrication—their uranium exports would attract the consent rights that those NSG participants might require.[49]

---

47. In addition, paragraph (a) of section 402 of the Nuclear Non-Proliferation Act of 1978 states, among other things, that, "except as specifically provided in any agreement for cooperation, no source or special nuclear material hereafter exported from the United States may be enriched after export without the prior approval of the United States for such enrichment."

48. Other countries with substantial uranium resources such as Jordan and Mongolia have not yet begun to export nuclear materials and do not belong to the NSG.

49. The United States, Eurodif (France and various other investors), Urenco (Germany, the Netherlands, and the United Kingdom), AREVA, and Russia are commercial suppliers of enrichment services.

Iran could be close to exhausting its supply of uranium and has reportedly been seeking to purchase uranium illegally on the international market for its enrichment program. UN Security Council resolutions ban exports to Iran of all "items, materials, equipment, goods and technology" that could contribute to its enrichment activities, including uranium ore. In addition, transfers of uranium ore in quantities greater than 500 kilograms annually are subject to the export control guidelines of the NSG. These restrictions effectively close the door on legal imports of significant quantities of uranium ore by Iran.

A consent right to enrichment remains an important nonproliferation tool, and its absence from the NSG guidelines remains a flaw that should be remedied. Suppliers have typically required consent to transfers and retransfers of uranium and low-enriched uranium to third countries, but the consent has often been given in advance to facilitate trade: because of a globalized supply chain, uranium conversion, fabrication, and enrichment are likely to take place in different countries so that advance consent is required. Also common is consent to enrich up to 20 percent in U-235, which is usually given in an agreement or export license. To date, suppliers have granted such consent only to existing holders of major enrichment technology, which are few in number. Moreover, at present only a few states possess enrichment capabilities, and even fewer have expressed an interest in acquiring such capability in the near term.

Consent Rights on Reprocessing, Alteration in Form or Content of Nuclear Material, and Storage of Weapons-Usable Nuclear Materials

Reprocessing plants separate plutonium from fission products, rendering the plutonium directly usable in nuclear weapons. Reprocessing facilities are also technically challenging to safeguard. The storage and use of plutonium, highly enriched uranium, and uranium-233 present proliferation risks because these materials are directly usable in nuclear weapons. Alteration in form or content also involves the handling or manipulation of weapons-usable nuclear material, such as plutonium fuel manufacture and, sometimes, postirradiation examination.[50]

China has two commercial-scale enrichment plants supplied by Russia to fuel its domestic civil nuclear reactors, while Argentina, India, Iran, Japan, and Pakistan have small enrichment capabilities. Brazil has plans to build an enrichment plant to meet its domestic reactor needs and has an enrichment plant to produce naval fuel. The facilities in India and Pakistan are unsafeguarded, and many believe that Iran's enrichment facilities, even though subject to safeguards by the IAEA, are intended for a nuclear-weapons option. The North Koreans recently revealed an enrichment plant to visiting American scientists, and there are indications that they may possess more than one such facility. Several nations have expressed an interest in acquiring a commercial enrichment capability at some time in the future, but there do not appear to be any states that have developed specific plans to build enrichment facilities in the near future with the possible exception of China. South Korea and South Africa have recently expressed an interest in acquiring enrichment capability.

50. U.S. law does not define the term *alteration in form or content*. However, most agreements expressly exclude the irradiation or further irradiation of plutonium from the definition of *alteration in form or con-*

UNITED STATES. U.S. agreements for peaceful nuclear cooperation must contain a guarantee by the cooperating country that it will not reprocess or otherwise alter in form or content U.S.-obligated nuclear material or store weapons-usable material—plutonium, highly enriched uranium, and uranium-233— without the prior approval of the United States.[51] It is important to note in this connection that the United States exercises its consent rights in accordance with the principle of proportionality in relation to produced plutonium. That is, when nuclear material of U.S. origin is combined with material not of U.S. origin and irradiated in a non-U.S.-supplied reactor, only the produced plutonium attributed to the material of U.S. origin is subject to U.S. consent rights. (For an explanation of the principle of proportionality, see the annex to this report.)

The United States has implemented its prior approval or right of consent for reprocessing, for alteration in form and content of U.S.-obligated nuclear materials, and for storage of weapons-usable materials in different ways, depending on the political and security relationship the United States has with its cooperating partners, the status of the partners' civil nuclear programs, their nonproliferation credentials, and the proliferation concerns in the regions in which they are located. In areas of regional instability or proliferation concern, the United States has required special restrictions on sensitive nuclear activities, specifically, in its agreements with Egypt and the United Arab Emirates.

> ***Limited Consent.*** In 1977, the United States gave its approval to Japan to reprocess a limited amount of spent fuel (99 tons) at its Tokai-Mura reprocessing plant for two years. This consent was extended and amended several times until it was replaced by the U.S.-Japan agreement for peaceful nuclear cooperation in 1988.
>
> ***Advance consent.*** As noted above, in the U.S. agreements with Norway and the UAE, the United States granted advance consent on a one-time basis to transfer U.S.-obligated spent fuel from these countries to EURATOM for reprocessing but retained consent rights over any subsequent disposition of the recovered plutonium and uranium.
>
> ***Programmatic consent.*** With a few cooperating partners that have advanced nuclear programs and comprehensive nonproliferation credentials, the United States has given so-called programmatic consent to reprocessing and other activities. The United States granted consent to reprocessing and the subsequent disposition of recovered plutonium in its agreements with Japan and EURATOM. The U.S. agreement with Switzerland pro-

---

tent. The term has generally been interpreted to include the manufacture of plutonium-bearing fuels in the case of power reactor fuel or HEU-bearing fuels in the case of research reactor fuel. This means that the United States must agree to the manufacture of plutonium (recovered from U.S.-obligated spent fuel) into mixed oxide fuel or to the manufacture of HEU into fuel elements or targets. In implementing U.S. agreements, the United States has treated the postirradiation examination of spent fuel in a pragmatic way. For example, if the cladding on irradiated fuel is changed in form or content, it is considered to be alteration in form or content. If the cladding is untouched, it is not considered to be alteration in form or content. Destructive testing of spent fuel is alteration in form or content, while nondestructive measurements of spent fuel are not. Refabrication of irradiated material recovered from destructive processing of spent fuel is alteration in form or content. In a few cases, *alteration in form or content* has been defined explicitly in an agreement. For example, in the U.S.-EURATOM Agreement, *alteration in form or content* means conversion of plutonium, highly enriched uranium, or uranium-233 or fabrication of fuel containing plutonium, highly enriched uranium, or uranium-233; it does not include postirradiation examination involving chemical dissolution or separation, disassembly or reassembly of fuel assemblies, irradiation, reprocessing, or enrichment.

51. See section 123 (a) (7) of the AEA.

vided consent to transfer U.S.-obligated spent fuel to EURATOM for reprocessing and the return of the recovered plutonium and uranium for use in designated Swiss civil nuclear facilities. The U.S. agreement with Japan also allowed for the retransfer of the recovered uranium and plutonium from EURATOM to Japan for use in its civil nuclear facilities. These consents were called "programmatic" because they were designed to meet the needs of the full fuel-cycle programs of the countries concerned, including the reprocessing of U.S.-obligated spent fuel and the storage of the recovered plutonium in facilities designated by the cooperating partner as constituting its civil nuclear program. In agreements with EURATOM, Japan, and Switzerland, the United States granted its consent once for the life of the respective agreements. The United States has also given advance consent to the reprocessing of U.S.-obligated spent fuel in safeguarded Indian reprocessing facilities (yet to be constructed) and the use of the recovered plutonium and uranium in safeguarded Indian reactors. In those agreements in which it has given advance or programmatic consent to reprocessing, the United States has the right to suspend its consent if it determines that exceptional concerns from a nonproliferation or a national security point of view require suspension. The agreements with EURATOM, Japan, and India contain language that calls for consultation concerning any suspension of consent and make clear that the United States may not exercise its rights of suspension for capricious or arbitrary reasons or for differences over the nature of a country's fuel-cycle program. The threshold for suspension of consent must be a determination that the continuation of the consent would present a serious threat to the security of the United States or result in a significant increase in the risk of proliferation. These suspension rights reflect a balance between the importance of giving the cooperating partner some degree of predictability while giving the United States the unilateral right to suspend its approval for serious reasons of national security or nonproliferation.

Special restrictions in regions of political instability and proliferation concern. The United States has taken special measures to ensure that U.S.-supplied materials are not used in sensitive nuclear activities in the Middle East. The U.S.-Egypt agreement for peaceful nuclear cooperation provides, among other things, that any reprocessing of U.S.-obligated nuclear material and any storage or fabrication of plutonium recovered as a result of such reprocessing will take place in facilities outside Egypt. The disposition of any resulting plutonium shall be subject to the mutual agreement of the parties. In the U.S.-UAE agreement for peaceful nuclear cooperation, the UAE agreed not to possess sensitive facilities for enrichment, reprocessing, or alteration in form or content. Violation of this provision could result in termination of U.S. cooperation under the agreement.

The agreements described above are not the norm for the U.S. approach to consent rights. For most of its cooperating partners, the United States discourages reprocessing and plutonium use, and most U.S. cooperating partners have neither requested nor been granted prior U.S. consent to reprocessing or alteration in form or content of spent fuel or enrichment of uranium. In a few cases, the United States has rebuffed informal requests for reprocessing.

U.S. law also specifies certain statutory criteria for granting U.S. approval for reprocessing. Specifically, section 131 of the AEA requires the secretary of energy to determine that the proposed reprocessing will "not be inimical to the common defense and security." In addition, the secretary of energy and the secretary of state must judge that reprocessing or retransfer for reprocessing "will not result in a significant increase in the risk of proliferation" beyond that which exists at the time the approval is requested. Section 131 also provides that

> among all the factors in making this judgment, foremost consideration will be given to whether or not the reprocessing or retransfer will take place under conditions that will ensure timely warning to the United States of any diversion well in advance of the time at which the non-nuclear-weapon state could transform the diverted material into a nuclear explosive device.

In practice, the interpretation of "timely warning" has been extremely complex. The law is silent as to what information and factors should be taken into account in considering and determining whether the timely warning standard is met. The legislative history does not make clear whether timely warning is the predominant factor or only the first in a list of factors. The executive branch has taken the position that the time it would take for a non-nuclear-weapon state to transform the diverted material into a nuclear explosive device could vary from case to case and that, "in view of the prominence accorded timely warning in the law, it is clear that a broad range of technical, political and other factors, including but not limited to safeguards and physical protection, can be relevant in detecting diversion and should be considered."[52]

TREATIES AND INTERNATIONAL AGREEMENTS

Nuclear Suppliers Group. Paragraph 8 of the guidelines states that suppliers should include in agreements for supply of nuclear materials or of facilities that produce material usable for nuclear weapons or other nuclear explosive devices provisions for mutual agreement between the supplier and the recipient on arrangements for reprocessing, storage, alteration, use, transfer, or retransfer of any material usable for nuclear weapons or other nuclear explosive devices involved. However, the language of the NSG guidelines does not impose an unqualified and unambiguous requirement for consent rights in all cases but merely calls for consent rights "whenever appropriate and practicable," leaving to the individual supplier how to interpret such a phrase.

OTHER COUNTRIES. The policies of most NSG suppliers on consent rights are less transparent than those of the United States, and there are gaps in knowledge about whether most states require consent rights on reprocessing, alteration in form and content, and storage in all cases and how they actually implement such rights. Policies and practices are not uniform among suppliers. Both Australia and Canada include these consent rights routinely in their bilateral agreements. The Australian and Canadian approaches to nuclear cooperation agreements have been influenced by and are very similar to U.S. practice. Australia and Canada gave programmatic consent to reprocessing to EURATOM and Japan. According to public knowledge, Australia and Canada have not given consent to reprocessing and to the storage or use of recovered plutonium to any other of their cooperating partners.

52. U.S. House of Representatives, "Proposed Agreement between the United States and Japan concerning Peaceful Uses of Nuclear Energy," 100th Congress, 1st sess., House Document 100-128, 369.

Other states have different policies toward consent rights for reprocessing and alteration in form or content. South Korea requires consent rights for reprocessing in its agreements with some countries but not others. Reportedly, it does not require consent rights in its cooperation with "advanced nuclear states" such as Argentina, Brazil, Canada, China, France, Germany, Russia, and the United Kingdom. Russia has been taking back spent fuel from its customers, but it is not known whether all Russian nuclear cooperation agreements contain explicit consent rights as recommended in the NSG guidelines. Moscow's agreement with the United States contains all the consent rights required by the NNPA on a reciprocal basis. Russia has never given its consent to any of its cooperating partners to the reprocessing or alteration in form or content of Russian-supplied nuclear material, to the storage or use of recovered plutonium, or to enrichment of the nuclear material it has supplied. Historically, Russia has prevented the reprocessing of Russian-supplied nuclear material by taking back spent fuel from some of its East European customers. Moscow has also agreed to take back the spent fuel produced in the Bushehr reactor made from Russian-supplied fuel and has recently offered similar arrangements to Vietnam and Turkey. It is not clear whether Russia will offer to take back spent fuel from other potential customers.

French policy is guided by the NSG guidelines and the European Declaration of Common Policy. French agreements do not generally contain consent rights for reprocessing because French policy is to take back the spent fuel produced from French-supplied nuclear materials for reprocessing in France. In its recently concluded agreement with India, it has granted New Delhi advance consent to reprocessing on essentially the same terms that the United States has approved Indian reprocessing of material subject to the U.S.-Indian agreement for peaceful nuclear cooperation. The United Kingdom also provides reprocessing services to other states but requires its customers to take back the recovered plutonium and uranium and the nuclear waste. However, plutonium returns have been made only to Japan and to states in Western Europe such as Germany and Switzerland.

Japan generally requires consent rights in its peaceful nuclear cooperation agreements. It has reciprocal consent rights on reprocessing, alteration in form or content, storage of plutonium, and enrichment (beyond 20 percent) in its agreements with the United States, Australia, and Canada. In its agreement with Russia, Japan has consent rights over reprocessing, enrichment, and retransfer of materials subject to its agreement with Russia. Japan's agreement with Kazakhstan contains consent rights only for retransfers to a third party. Japan's agreement with South Korea contains consent rights on enrichment over 20 percent and reprocessing. Japan's agreements with Jordan and Vietnam prohibit the reprocessing of nuclear materials subject to the agreements with each country.

The agreements in which suppliers have given programmatic consent to reprocessing, such as the Australian and Canadian agreements with EURATOM and Japan and the Russian agreement with India, contain general provisions for termination of cooperation if the cooperating partner violates the agreement or IAEA safeguards. However, unlike U.S. agreements in which the United States has given similar programmatic consent to reprocessing and plutonium use, they do not explicitly contain a unilateral supplier right to suspend such consent for reasons of nonproliferation and national security.

Whereas the NSG guidelines on prior consent are not legal commitments and call for such consent rights whenever "appropriate and practicable," U.S. law requires that all U.S. agreements for peaceful nuclear cooperation contain prior consent rights over reprocessing and alteration in form or content of U.S.-obligated nuclear material, storage of weapons-usable materials, enrichment of U.S.-supplied nuclear materials, and retransfer of nuclear materials and equipment subject to U.S. agreements. (The United States regards the consent rights as applying to all future generations of plutonium used in or produced through the use of U.S.-obligated nuclear material and equipment. It is not known whether other suppliers regard their consent rights as applying to future generations of plutonium.)

In practice, only a few suppliers (the United States, Australia, and Canada) have actually given consent to reprocessing or to plutonium storage and use and then only to a small number of countries, namely, those in EURATOM, Japan, Switzerland, and India. The reprocessing that has taken place outside these areas has largely been the result of indigenous development and has not involved imported nuclear materials. North Korea, Israel, Pakistan, Argentina, and Brazil possess their own reprocessing capabilities, have largely used their own nuclear materials in these programs, and have not sought the prior consent of supplier states to use imported materials for such purposes.

As more countries embark on new nuclear programs and express interest in reprocessing either for purposes of plutonium recycling or waste management, consent rights for reprocessing could be an important tool, in conjunction with technology controls and fuel-cycle incentives, in discouraging the spread of enrichment and reprocessing facilities.

Retroactivity of Nonproliferation Conditions

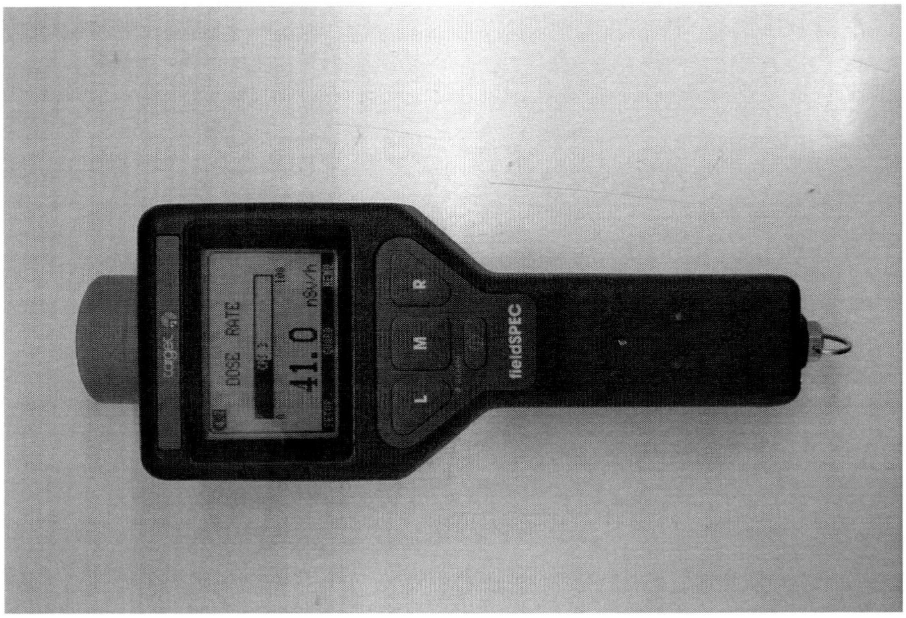

Portable analyzers such as this are used by inspectors to measure the level of energy emitted by radioactive sources. Credit: Dean Calma/IAEA 2002. http://www.iaea.org/NewsCenter/Multimedia/Imagebank/index.jsp.

UNITED STATES. Although not required by law, the U.S. government applies the nonproliferation controls contained in post-NNPA agreements for peaceful nuclear cooperation retroactively to the nuclear materials and equipment covered by the previous agreements that they replaced. Therefore, nuclear material that had been subject to a previous agreement has become subject to the full panoply of assurances and controls of the new post-NNPA agreement. The effect of this provision is to add new NNPA-mandated nonproliferation controls over and above those that existed in the old agreements. Nuclear material that had been free of certain U.S. consent rights under an old agreement is now subject retroactively to those consent rights under the post-NNPA agreement. It is not known whether any other nuclear suppliers have adopted similar approaches.

The NSG guidelines do not provide for retroactivity of nonproliferation controls, and it is not clear whether individual suppliers have policies on retroactivity similar to U.S. requirements.

Perpetuity of Nonproliferation Controls

A close-up view of the broken seals salvaged from DPRK facilities. Safeguards inspectors use metal seals to tag safeguarded equipment at nuclear facilities. Credit: Kirstie Hansen/IAEA 2003. http://www.iaea.org/NewsCenter/Multimedia/Imagebank/index.jsp.

UNITED STATES. Although not required by U.S. law, all the nonproliferation conditions and controls in U.S. agreements for peaceful nuclear cooperation continue in effect even if the agreements terminate, expire, or are suspended. Post-NNPA agreements explicitly provide that these obligations continue in effect as long as the nuclear material and equipment subject to the agreement remain in the territory of the cooperating partner or under its jurisdiction or control anywhere, or until such time as the United States and the country concerned agree that the nuclear material is no longer usable for any nuclear activity relevant from the point of view of safeguards.

TREATIES AND INTERNATIONAL AGREEMENTS

Nuclear Suppliers Group. The NSG guidelines provide for the perpetuity of safeguards but not for the other nonproliferation guarantees and assurances contained in the guidelines.

Any differences that may exist between the policies of United States and those of other major nuclear powers on the perpetuity of all nonproliferation controls have had no practical implications thus far, but the NSG would do well to adopt a policy similar to that of the United States.

Dual-Use Export Controls

An IAEA action team inspector uncovers a CNC machine tool, a piece of technology used to manufacture centrifuge components. Credit: Action Team 1991-1998/ IAEA 1991. http://www.iaea.org/NewsCenter/Multimedia/Imagebank/index.jsp.

Some equipment, materials, software, and related technology are not designed or prepared solely for nuclear purposes but may have both nuclear and nonnuclear applications. These dual-use items and technology could make a major contribution to a nuclear explosive activity, an unsafeguarded nuclear fuel-cycle activity, or acts of nuclear terrorism.[53]

UNITED STATES. The United States has long controlled the exports of dual-use items and technology, that is, those that have both civil and military nuclear uses. Dual-use items and technology do not require an agreement for cooperation or an export license from the Nuclear Regulatory Commission. Section 309 (c) of the NNPA directs the Department of Commerce to control all export items other than those licensed by the NRC that could be of significance for nuclear explosive purposes.

TREATIES AND INTERNATIONAL AGREEMENTS

Nuclear Suppliers Group. The United States called attention to the problem of dual-use exports throughout the 1980s and by 1990 had begun to urge other states to agree on some kind of multilateral control system for such items. At the 1990 NPT Review Conference, the committee dealing with article III of the treaty recommended appropriate coordination among suppliers to control dual-use items. However, it was the revelations surrounding Iraq's nuclear-weapons program in 1991 that dramatically demonstrated the need for a multilateral system of export controls for dual-use items. In April 1992,

53. As used in this report, the term dual-use is meant to encompass materials, equipment, components, and technology that have both nuclear and nonnuclear uses. Dual-use is not meant in the sense that some nuclear technologies such as an enrichment plant may make enriched uranium either to fuel a civil power reactor for the production of electricity or to make a nuclear weapon.

the NSG adopted a new regime to control exports of nuclear-related dual-use materials, equipment, and technology. The dual-use arrangement consisted of a set of guidelines for transfers of some 65 dual-use items, including equipment, materials, and technology. The dual-use guidelines call for suppliers not to transfer dual-use items on the list under certain conditions: (1) if they are to be used in nuclear explosive activities or in an unsafeguarded nuclear fuel cycle; (2) if there is an unacceptable risk of their diversion to such activities; or (3) if their transfer would be contrary to the objective of averting the proliferation of nuclear weapons. The dual-use arrangement also identifies the factors that suppliers should consider in assessing recipients' nonproliferation standing and conditions on transfers and retransfers. These include, for example, whether the recipient is a party to the NPT; whether it has an IAEA safeguards agreement in force; whether the equipment, materials, software, or related technology to be transferred is appropriate for the stated end-use and whether that stated end-use is appropriate for the end-user; whether the equipment, materials, software, or related technology to be transferred is to be used in research on or the development, design, manufacture, construction, operation, or maintenance of any reprocessing or enrichment facility; and whether the recipients have been engaged in clandestine or illegal procurement activities. The dual-use arrangements were published by the IAEA in July 1992 as INFCIRC/254/ Part 2. The Nuclear Referral List of the Department of Commerce is revised from time to time and is kept in harmony with the list of dual-use items in the NSG guidelines.

In addition to the new NSG guidelines, various individual states have implemented new laws and regulations to control dual-use exports. The German government in particular has greatly strengthened its export controls and enforcement procedures. Among other things, German law requires that each company introduce an internal compliance system and nominate a senior executive who would be held personally accountable for the implementation of his company's export decisions.[54]

During the 1980s, some countries intent on developing their own nuclear weapons—in particular, Iraq and Pakistan—were successful in obtaining dual-use technology on the international market that made a significant contribution to their nuclear explosive efforts. These countries obtained such items by exploiting the lack of suppliers' national export regulations on dual-use items and by employing various means of clandestine procurement such as using their embassies as well as front companies and multiple intermediaries, false end-use statements, and transshipment through third countries. They found it easier to procure subcomponents and equipment to construct major components themselves than to obtain the items that were listed on supplier Trigger-Lists. Thus, an important key to the success of these efforts was the weakness of Western export controls, since most suppliers did not have in place legislation or regulations that controlled the export of dual-use equipment and materials. (One major exception was

54. David Albright, "Preventing Illegal Exports: Learning from Case Studies" Institute for Science and International Security, Part I, April 6, 2001, http://isis-online.org/conferences/detail/preventing-illegal-exports-learning-from-case-studies/20.

the United States.) The failure of the major suppliers, with that one exception, to control dual-use items and technology proved to be a major vulnerability in nuclear export controls. The irony is that while the United States and the NSG members had put in place rigorous export controls on nuclear materials, equipment, and technology, the absence of adequate controls on less sensitive dual-use items proved to be the principal source of nuclear proliferation during the 1980s.

Catch-All Controls

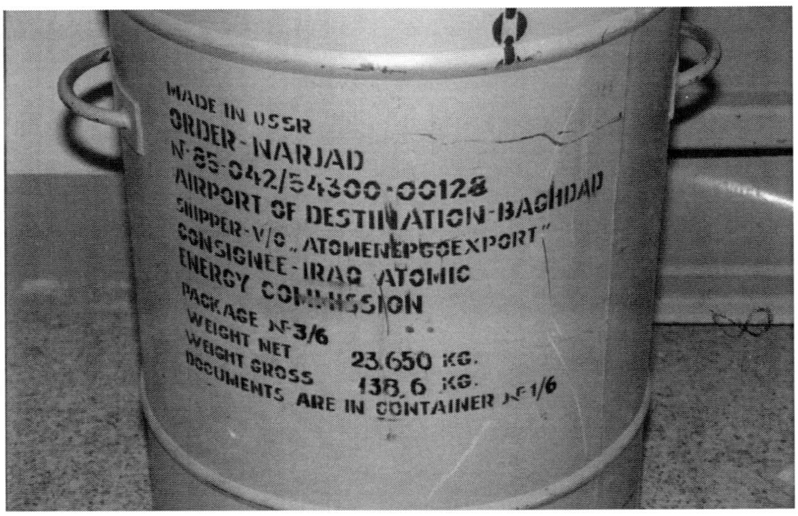

Evidence of Saddam's secret nuclear program. A drum of radioactive material discovered in Iraq in 1991. Credit: Action Team 1991-1998/IAEA 1991. http://www.iaea.org/NewsCenter/Multimedia/Imagebank/index.jsp.

Catch-all clauses are important to the nonproliferation regime because they allow supplier states to prevent exports of any item, whether it is on an export control list or not, that is intended for a nuclear-weapons program. For example, states do not control the export of air conditioning equipment. Yet air conditioning is essential to the operation of a uranium centrifuge enrichment plant. The catch-all clause thus enables export authorities to prevent the export of fairly common items that are not on any export control list but that can make an important contribution to facilities dedicated to producing nuclear explosive devices.

UNITED STATES. The United States has had a catch-all clause in its export regulations since the early 1980s. The Department of Commerce has the authority to require that any item be exported under a license even if that item is not on any control list, if the exporter knows that the item will be used for nuclear explosive activities, unsafeguarded nuclear activities, or safeguarded nuclear activities involving reprocessing, heavy water production, enrichment, or plutonium fuel fabrication. The regulations governing these catch-all controls are found in Export Administration Regulations Part 744.

Nuclear Suppliers Group. At its May 2004 meeting, the NSG decided to adopt a catch-all mechanism to provide a national legal basis for controlling the export of nuclear-related items that are not on any export control lists, when such items are or may be intended for use in connection with a nuclear explosive activity.

The U.S. catch-all controls are directed at a broader range of activities than those of the NSG. The NSG catch-all clause is triggered only if the proposed dual-use export is intended for nuclear explosive purposes, while the U.S. provision applies not only to nuclear explosives but also to unsafeguarded nuclear activities or safeguarded nuclear activities involving reprocessing, heavy water production, enrichment, or plutonium fuel fabrication. It is not known whether the disparity in U.S. and NSG policies has had any practical effect. Moreover, it is extremely difficult to gauge the effectiveness of catch-all clauses, since procurement efforts by nuclear aspirants are usually clandestine in nature, and only attempted purchases for nuclear explosive programs that have been successfully interdicted can be observed.

Termination of Nuclear Cooperation

Y-12 security police officer guards components of a Libyan gas centrifuge for enriching uranium that were surrendered to the United States and shipped to Y12. Credit: Y-12 National Security Complex 2004. http://www.y12.doe.gov/news/report/toc.php?vn=1_1&xml=f1.

The credibility of the nonproliferation regime could not be preserved if a country that violates its nonproliferation obligations is allowed to continue to enjoy the benefits of peaceful nuclear commerce. Therefore, a supplier's right to terminate nuclear cooperation with a country that does not comply with its nonproliferation commitments is an essential tool for preserving the integrity and effectiveness of the nonproliferation regime.

UNITED STATES. The AEA (section 129) provides that no nuclear materials and equipment or sensitive nuclear technology shall be exported to

> (1) Any non-nuclear-weapon state that is found by the President to have, at any time after the effective date of this section (March 10, 1978): (A) detonated a nuclear explosive device; or (B) terminated or abrogated IAEA safeguards; or (C) materially violated an IAEA safeguards agreement; or (D) engaged in activities involving source or special nuclear material and having direct significance for the manufacture or acquisition of nuclear explosive devices, and has failed to take steps which, in the President's judgment, represent sufficient progress toward terminating such activities; or
>
> (2) any nation or group of nations that is found by the President to have, at any time after the effective date of this section, (A) materially violated an agreement for cooperation with the United States, or, with respect to material or equipment not supplied under an agreement for cooperation, materially violated the terms under which such material or equipment was supplied or the terms of any commitments obtained with respect thereto pursuant to section 402 (a) of the Nuclear Non-Proliferation Act of 1978; or (B) assisted, encouraged, or induced any non-nuclear-weapon state to engage in activities involving source of special nuclear material and having direct significance for the manufacture or acquisition of nuclear explosive devices, and has failed to take steps which, in the President's judgment, represent sufficient progress toward terminating such assistance, encouragement or inducement; or (C) entered into an agreement after the date of enactment of this section for the transfer of reprocessing equipment, materials, or technology to the sovereign control of any non-nuclear-weapon state except in connection with an international fuel-cycle evaluation in which the United States is a participant or pursuant to a subsequent international agreement or understanding to which the United States subscribes.

This provision of the law allows the president to waive this requirement and to permit the continuation of nuclear exports if he determines that a cessation of nuclear cooperation would be prejudicial to the achievement of U.S. nonproliferation objectives or otherwise jeopardize the common defense and security of the United States. However, before the effective date of any such determination, the president must submit the determination, together with a report containing the reasons for his determination, to foreign affairs committees of both houses of Congress for 60 days of continuous session. The United States has never implemented section 129 of the AEA to terminate nuclear exports to any of its cooperating partners.

TREATIES AND INTERNATIONAL AGREEMENTS

> ***Nuclear Suppliers Group.*** Paragraph16 (c) of the NSG guidelines states that suppliers should consult in the event that one or more of them believe that there has been a violation of the supplier-recipient understanding resulting from these guidelines, particularly in the case of an explosion of a nuclear device, or if there has been an illegal termination or violation of IAEA safeguards by a recipient. The guidelines also recommend that each supplier also consider suspending transfers of Trigger-List items while consultations are ongoing, pending supplier agreement on an appropriate response. Upon the findings of

such consultations, the suppliers, bearing in mind article XII of the IAEA statute, should agree on an appropriate response and possible action, which could include the termination of nuclear transfers to that recipient. According to paragraph16 (d), if the IAEA finds that a recipient is in breach of its obligation to comply with its safeguards agreement, suppliers should consider the suspension of the transfer of Trigger-List items to that state while it is under investigation by the IAEA. Paragraph16 (e) requires suppliers to support the suspension of transfers of Trigger-List items to states that violate their nuclear nonproliferation and safeguards obligations, recognizing that the responsibility and authority for such decisions rest with national governments or the UN Security Council. In particular, such suspension is applicable in situations in which the IAEA Board of Governors finds that a state has been in noncompliance with a safeguards agreement or decides that the agency is not able to verify that there has been no diversion of safeguarded nuclear material.

However, the NSG guidelines contain an important exception to terminating nuclear cooperation. They provide that suspension of the supply of Trigger-List items would not apply if such items are deemed essential for the safe operation of existing facilities and if safeguards are applied to those facilities.

There have been some instances when suppliers terminated nuclear cooperation with customers for reasons of nonproliferation. For example, Canada ended nuclear trade with India after New Delhi used the reactor supplied by Ottawa for its nuclear test in 1974. The United States terminated nuclear cooperation with Argentina, Brazil, and India after 1980 when the NNPA's requirement for comprehensive safeguards took effect. France ended its supply of enriched uranium for the Tarapur reactor after it joined the NPT in 1992 as did China when it joined the NSG in 2004. China halted its plans for nuclear supplies to Iran in 1998 at the urging of the United States. On the whole, however, the international nuclear market has operated smoothly with few interruptions of supply.

The grounds for U.S. termination of nuclear cooperation are more extensive than those set out by the NSG. U.S. law also obliges the president to terminate nuclear cooperation once he determines that the recipient has violated certain defined conditions but does allow the president to waive termination if he determines it would be damaging to U.S. nonproliferation interests. The NSG guidelines, in contrast, provide only for consultation in the event of a violation and state only that NSG members should consider suspension of exports of Trigger-List items. Moreover, the guidelines tie such suspension to decisions by the IAEA Board of Governors, while the U.S. law is dependent solely on a determination by the president. Finally, the United States provides for no "safety" exception, while the NSG suspension provisions would not apply if continued exports of Trigger-List items are deemed essential for safety reasons.

Right of Return

Transport of spent fuel. A spent fuel flask is loaded and secured into the ship for domestic sea movement in Japan. Credit: John Mairs/IAEA 1992. http://www.iaea.org/NewsCenter/Multimedia/Imagebank/index.jsp.

UNITED STATES. U.S. law—AEA 123 (a) (4)—requires that peaceful nuclear cooperation agreements contain a U.S. right to require the return of U.S.-obligated nuclear material and equipment, if the cooperating partner detonates a nuclear explosive device or terminates or abrogates an IAEA safeguards agreement. As a matter of policy, the United States typically expands the right of return in U.S. agreements for peaceful nuclear cooperation to include other triggering events such as violation of the U.S. agreement.

TREATIES AND INTERNATIONAL AGREEMENTS

Nuclear Suppliers Group. Paragraph 4 (9) (a) of the NSG guidelines provide that "if the IAEA decides that the application of IAEA safeguards is no longer possible, the supplier and recipient should elaborate appropriate verification measures. If the recipient does not accept these measures, it should allow at the request of the supplier the restitution of transferred and derived Trigger-List items." This guideline does not apply to agreements or contracts drawn up on or before April 3, 1992. It is not known whether other suppliers have incorporated this requirement in new agreements for peaceful nuclear cooperation.

UN Security Council Resolution 1887. Resolution 1887 "Encourages States to require as a condition of nuclear exports that the recipient State agree that, in the event that it should terminate, withdraw from, or be found by the IAEA Board of Governors to be in non-compliance with its IAEA safeguards agreement, the supplier state would have a right to require the return of nuclear material and equipment provided prior to such termination, non-compliance or withdrawal, as well as any special nuclear material produced through the use of such material or equipment."

The grounds for exercising the U.S. right of return are much more extensive than those of the NSG. However, neither the United States nor any other supplier has ever exercised a right of return. Moreover, even if the United States determined that the circumstances noted above justified the exercise of such a right, it would encounter major legal and political obstacles to bringing some nuclear materials, such as a power reactor's spent fuel or irradiated equipment or components, into the country. The United States and other suppliers would probably face formidable obstacles, including public opposition to storage of such materials. Thus, the right of return is largely symbolic.

3 AGENDA FOR THE FUTURE

Most of the states that have acquired nuclear weapons have done so not by diverting materials or technology from their civil nuclear programs or from peaceful international nuclear commerce, but from dedicated military programs. Most acquired their nuclear-weapons capability by obtaining direct and deliberate assistance from a nuclear-weapon state, by stealing classified or sensitive nuclear technology, or by clandestinely and illicitly procuring key equipment and technology on the international market. A major exception was India, when it violated its nonproliferation undertakings with Canada and the United States to manufacture its nuclear explosive device in 1974.[55]

Nonetheless, peaceful nuclear commerce has also been exploited to advance nuclear explosives programs. Some supplier states have in the past acted irresponsibly by placing commercial or strategic considerations above nonproliferation interests. A few continue to do so today. In the 1970s, France entered into contracts to sell reprocessing plants to Pakistan, South Korea, and Taiwan before backing out of these deals later in the decade. Also in the 1970s, Germany entered into contracts to sell enrichment and reprocessing technology to Brazil.[56] In the 1980s, Germany sold reactors to Argentina in the absence of comprehensive safeguards.[57] The failure of European and other countries to control dual-use exports until the early 1990s contributed significantly to the nuclear-weapons programs of Pakistan and Iraq. These states successfully used clandestine techniques to obtain technology from other countries to build a nuclear-weapons capacity. In the 1990s, the United States had to intervene to dissuade Russia from allowing the transfer of sensitive nuclear technology to Iran.

In addition, some states have undermined the international consensus on requiring comprehensive IAEA safeguards as a condition of supply. As discussed above, the NSG guidelines contain two exceptions that have proved to be significant loopholes: the so-called grandfather and the safety clauses were used by Russia and China to supply nuclear reactors and fuel to India and Pakistan—two non-NPT parties without comprehensive safeguards. The United States for its own strategic and commercial reasons put a dagger into the heart of the comprehensive safeguards norm by entering into a peaceful nuclear cooperation agreement with India without insisting on

55. The IAEA has also found several states in noncompliance with their safeguards agreements—Iran, Iraq, Libya, North Korea, Romania, and Syria.

56. In December 1976, the French government announced that it had decided to no longer authorize—until further notice—bilateral contracts pertaining to the sale to third countries of industrial facilities for spent fuel reprocessing. In June 1977, the German government issued a declaration to the effect that it would not grant any license for the export of reprocessing facilities until further notice. Subsequent governments have reaffirmed this commitment. Although there has never been a similar pronouncement regarding enrichment, German government officials have indicated that it was safe to assume that what was said about reprocessing applies to enrichment, too.

57. Argentina did not ratify the NPT until 1995.

India placing all its nuclear activities under IAEA safeguards and then by persuading the NSG to approve an exemption for India from the NSG comprehensive safeguards requirement. Now Pakistan is seeking comparable benefits from the United States and the NSG.

The selective interpretation of NSG guidelines for exempting a recipient state does not bode well for the effectiveness of the export control regimes of the major nuclear suppliers. These actions can only lead to charges of hypocrisy and undermine the regime's legitimacy in the eyes of nonmembers.

Nuclear export control policies cannot solve or even address all proliferation challenges. In the past, states such as Russia (in the case of China), France (in the case of Israel), and China (in the case of Pakistan) have deliberately undermined the nonproliferation regime by assisting other states in acquiring or manufacturing nuclear weapons. Moreover, even the most effective nuclear export policies of the major suppliers cannot prevent the irresponsible behavior of nonmembers such as Pakistan or North Korea from undermining the effectiveness of international nuclear export controls and of the nonproliferation regime itself. Such cases have to be addressed through other means such as vigorous diplomatic pressure, sanctions, interdiction measures such as the Proliferation Security Initiative, or, in the extreme and where justified, preemptive military actions.

Nevertheless, the nuclear export policies of the major nuclear suppliers has had some success in increasing the costs and risks of the procurement efforts of such states as Pakistan, Iran, and Iraq and in delaying their acquisition of sensitive nuclear facilities or nuclear weapons. Moreover, if the major suppliers had not forged an agreement on common rules of the game, supplier states would have been tempted to further their competitive position in the international market by minimizing the nonproliferation conditions on their nuclear exports.

The export policies of the United States and other major suppliers must remain an essential component of the nonproliferation regime for a number of reasons:

- They provide an essential complement to the NPT without violating the rights of the parties to the treaty. The NPT constitutes the indispensable, albeit imperfect, foundation of the international nonproliferation regime. By requiring comprehensive and fall-back safeguards, physical protection, rules for technology transfers, controls on dual-use items, and sanctions for violations of nonproliferation norms, nuclear export controls have bolstered the effectiveness of the nonproliferation regime in essential ways that the NPT cannot do by itself.
- They serve as legal and normative barriers to the misuse of civil nuclear programs for nuclear explosive or military uses.
- They provide a basis for terminating nuclear cooperation and the imposition of international sanctions if a recipient violates nonproliferation norms and commitments.
- They can increase the costs and risks of the procurement efforts of such states as nuclear-weapon aspirants and in delaying their acquisition of sensitive nuclear facilities or nuclear weapons.
- Finally, they are necessary to upholding two basic principles of the nonproliferation regime: first, that states that wish to benefit from international cooperation in the peaceful uses of nuclear energy must make effective commitments to forswear the misuse of that technology for nuclear explosive or military purposes and to accept adequate verification

> of those commitments; and, second, international peaceful nuclear cooperation cannot take place unless the public and the national governments have confidence that it is taking place on a firm basis of nonproliferation assurances designed to prevent the diversion of civil nuclear programs to explosive purposes.

Nuclear export controls have evolved over time to keep pace with technical innovations and political developments and in response to various challenges to the nonproliferation regime. As a result, they are much better positioned than they have been in the past to block the international procurement efforts of aspiring nuclear-weapon states and to prevent the diversion of global nuclear commerce to nuclear explosive uses.

What Next?

Still more needs to be done. Nuclear-supplier states have a special responsibility for and interest in supporting an effective international nonproliferation regime. Such a regime is necessary to assure the public and national governments that international commerce in civil nuclear energy is being effectively controlled and that proliferation risks associated with the atom are manageable. In the absence of such confidence, governments will not license nuclear exports and imports, the public will oppose the development of nuclear power, and the nuclear industry will not accept the risk of investment in nuclear technology. The major nuclear suppliers need to adopt new and strengthened export controls to keep pace with the emerging nonproliferation challenges ahead. Among the most pressing are those that follow.

ENSURING INTEGRITY AND COMMONALITY OF EXPORT CONTROLS. Ensuring that supplier states have common policies for nuclear export control is vital to dissuading nuclear-exporting states from competing with each other on the international market by resorting to the lowest common denominator in nonproliferation requirements. Without an agreement on common rules of the game, supplier states will be at the very least tempted to further their competitive position by minimizing the nonproliferation conditions of their nuclear exports. Nuclear aspirants will be able to play one supplier off against another to obtain nuclear equipment and technology on minimal nonproliferation terms. This is precisely what happened in the 1980s, when Argentina decided to purchase nuclear facilities from the Federal Republic of Germany and Switzerland rather than Canada because Ottawa required comprehensive safeguards as a condition of export. Having some common understanding on export controls was and remains necessary to reducing the incentive of the major supplier states to weaken nonproliferation controls as a means of competing in the international nuclear marketplace, a development that could lead to the unraveling of the global nonproliferation regime.

In general, the United States has a more stringent and more encompassing set of nonproliferation conditions than other suppliers. In the past, this disparity had a significant impact particularly when many other suppliers did not require comprehensive safeguards or dual-use export controls. These differences allowed such countries as Argentina and Brazil to benefit from the peaceful uses of nuclear energy while pursuing unsafeguarded or nuclear-weapons activities. More important, the disparities in export control laws enabled such countries as Pakistan and Iraq to purchase dual-use items critical to their nuclear-weapons programs on the international market. As the NSG has adopted new and strengthened guidelines, it is not clear whether remaining disparities in laws, policies, and regulations and in the resources devoted to implementing them are having any practical impact at present. However, when a state such as China seeks to exploit loopholes in or adopt loose interpretations of the NSG guidelines, it threatens the global nuclear export control regime. Thus, one of the main objectives of the United States and other members of the NSG should be to hold China accountable for not requiring comprehensive safeguards as a condition of supply on its exports to Pakistan.

STRENGTHENING SAFEGUARDS. Nuclear-supplier states should take the initiative to ensure that the IAEA has the financial, political, and technical support it needs to implement an effective safeguards system. The NSG could also help improve the IAEA safeguards system significantly by requiring recipient states to put into effect the Additional Protocol as a condition of supply. Universal adoption of the AP is necessary for giving the IAEA the critical additional authority to detect clandestine nuclear activities. While many states have adopted the AP, it has been on a voluntary basis. Requiring the AP as a condition of supply will make it mandatory and help make it the widely accepted IAEA safeguards standard. Participating states will probably not be willing to accept this new guideline unless it is made prospective rather than retrospective. Nevertheless, forging NSG agreement on requiring the AP as a condition of supply must be a high priority of the United States and other major suppliers. In addition, suppliers should follow the recommendations of the *Report of the Commission of Eminent Persons on the Future of the Agency*,[58] which concluded that "all member states should provide the IAEA with the information it needs to do its job—including data on exports and imports of nuclear and related technologies, export denials, inquiries, and suspicious procurement attempts; information that states may have available from other sources; relevant police information, as appropriate; and more."

PREVENTING THE SPREAD OF ENRICHMENT AND REPROCESSING. Preventing the spread of enrichment and reprocessing technology has been a high-profile and highly contentious issue for some time. The NSG debated restraints on the transfer of enrichment and reprocessing for some seven years before agreeing on a new set of criteria. The members of the NSG soundly rejected the Bush administration's proposal to ban enrichment and reprocessing transfers to countries that do not already possess such capabilities. The members of the NSG have now adopted a criteria-based approach to the transfer of these sensitive nuclear technologies, and the NSG is highly unlikely to expand these controls for the foreseeable future. Moreover, major nuclear suppliers are unlikely to adopt formal rules banning transfers of enrichment and reprocessing or to insist that recipient states denounce the acquisition of either technology as the United States has done with the UAE. However, what the major nuclear suppliers actually do in practice is important, not the formal rules or guidelines they write. And they are in fact doing what the Bush administration proposed in 2004—refraining from exporting technology to countries that do not already possess such capability. While enrichment and reprocessing transfer continues to be a topic of considerable discussion in the U.S. Congress and in U.S. nonproliferation circles, this is a less pressing issue than others, since, for one thing, no NSG members are now transferring such technologies except to states that already possess enrichment and reprocessing capabilities and, for another, few states are actually seeking such technologies. Restrictions on transfers of enrichment and reprocessing remain a key but limited tool in minimizing the risks of civil nuclear commerce. They need to be reinforced with incentives such as the continued availability of an efficient enrichment services market, back-up fuel supply assurances, and the offer of spent fuel management services.

58. IAEA Board of Governors General Conference (GOV/200822-GC (52) INF/4), "Report of the Commission of Eminent Persons on the Future of the Agency," May 23, 2008, http://www.iaea.org/About/Policy/GC/GC52/GC52InfDocuments/English/gc52inf-4_en.pdf.

LIMITING AND ELIMINATING THE USE OF HIGHLY ENRICHED URANIUM. Suppliers should devote the resources necessary to developing technologies that do not rely on HEU for research or medical isotope production. In the meantime, they should adopt export policies that tie the export of HEU to a commitment by the recipient to convert from HEU to LEU fuel for research reactors and to commit to eliminating HEU from international commerce.

UNIVERSALITY OF NUCLEAR TRADE RULES. Many states do not adhere to the guidelines of the NSG or the ZC but have the capability of providing significant types of assistance to a nuclear explosives program. Often, these states do not have the legal or regulatory regimes, the resources, or, in some cases, the will to implement effective nuclear export controls. A primary goal of the major suppliers should be to persuade these states to adopt responsible nuclear export policies, perhaps by convincing them either to join the ZC or the NSG or to abide by their guidelines. Persuading uranium producers like Namibia and Niger to adopt effective export controls would be a significant strengthening of the nonproliferation regime as would be a well-coordinated effort to assist states that do not belong to the NSG or ZC in establishing the legal, regulatory, and enforcement mechanisms to implement effective nuclear and dual-use export control mechanisms. The UN Security Council's adoption of Resolution 1540 in 2004 was an important step in obligating states that are not members of the ZC or NSG to establish effective export controls. That resolution calls on states to put in place "appropriate effective measures to account for and secure" items related to weapons of mass destruction in production, use, storage, or transport and to "maintain appropriate effective physical protection measures" of said items. The primary purpose was to deny such items to non-state actors, but it does hold states accountable for their export controls. The United States and other major nuclear suppliers should play a major role in helping such states put into effect adequate export control systems.

REQUIRING CONSENT RIGHTS OVER ENRICHMENT. While the NSG guidelines call for a consent right on reprocessing, they do not provide for a consent right on enrichment. This is an important flaw that needs to be corrected.

REQUIRING PERPETUITY OF ALL NONPROLIFERATION CONTROLS. The NSG should follow the example of the United States and extend its guideline on the perpetuity of international safeguards to all nonproliferation controls and guarantees contained in the guidelines.

IMPROVING PHYSICAL PROTECTION. U.S. and other supplier policies require the application of physical protection measures to the nuclear materials they export. However, the criteria they require are those specified in the CPPNM and the NSG, which are quite general in nature and leave to the individual recipient state the responsibility of how to implement those obligations. The IAEA recommendations on physical protection (INFCIRC/225) are a far superior basis for physical protection requirements. Recent U.S. agreements for peaceful nuclear cooperation require recipient states to apply measures of physical protection in accordance with their national legislation that meets levels not less than the recommendations of the IAEA's current document INFCIRC/225 or in any revision or replacement of that document. The United States should continue this practice in future agreements, and other suppliers should follow suit. The NSG does not now impose any requirement that suppliers verify the adequacy of a recipient state's physical protection system. The United States has had the practice of conducting physical protection visits to and exchanging information on best practices with states that possess weapons-usable materials of U.S.-origin. The United States and the other major nuclear exporters may wish to consider requiring that a recipient state, as a condition of nuclear supply, invite the IAEA to conduct a peer review of its physical protection laws, regulations, and measures.[59] However, attaining this objective may prove formidable, given the sensitivities that states have about preserving physical protection as a national responsibility and fears of revealing sensitive security measures to international reviewers.

PREVENTING CLANDESTINE PROCUREMENT. States such as Pakistan, Iran, Iraq, and North Korea have enjoyed considerable success in the clandestine procurement of items for their nuclear-weapons programs. Iran and North Korea continue to try to exploit weaknesses in the export control system of major nuclear suppliers. It will, therefore, be important for the major suppliers to stay ahead of the often clever and ingenious methods such states use to acquire items on the international market that they need to support their nuclear-weapons ambitions. Nuclear-exporting states must ensure that they have established adequate laws and regulations and devote the necessary resources to implementing them effectively, and they must share information with each other about clandestine procurement efforts.

UPDATING LISTS OF CONTROLLED ITEMS. A 2006 Office of U.S. Government Accountability (GAO) report[60] concluded that NSG members did not promptly review and agree upon common lists of items to control and approaches to controlling them. Each member must make changes to its national export control policies after members agree to change items on the control list. If agreed changes to control lists are not adopted at the same time by all members, proliferators could exploit these time lags to obtain sensitive technologies by focusing on members that are slowest to incorporate the changes. As a result, sensitive items may still be traded to countries of concern. The GAO concluded that the rapid pace of nuclear technological change and the growing trade of sensitive items among proliferators complicate efforts to keep control lists current. The NSG is in the process of updating its export control lists and needs to do so more frequently.

PROMOTING LEGITIMACY. Some nonproliferation advocates have lamented the fact that article IV of the NPT affirms the "inalienable right of all the Parties to the Treaty to develop research, production and use of nuclear energy for peaceful purposes without discrimination and in conformity with Articles I and II of this Treaty" and affirms that "all the Parties to the Treaty undertake to facilitate, and have the right to participate in, the fullest possible exchange of equipment, materials and scientific and technological information for the peaceful uses of nuclear energy." However, it is important to recall that non-nuclear-weapon states would never have accepted international safeguards and nonexplosive-use pledges without receiving the quid pro quo contained in article IV of the NPT. Moreover, the right to peaceful uses of nuclear energy recognized in the NPT is not unconditional but is dependent on a state's adherence to its nonproliferation obligations. Article IV does not oblige suppliers to provide a particular kind of technology such as enrichment and reprocessing to nonnuclear states party to the treaty. However, suppliers need to take account of the fact that many non-nuclear-weapon states, particularly developing countries,

59. The IAEA already has programs to train member states in establishing physical protection systems and upon request to inspect and review member states' efforts to provide physical protection of their nuclear materials and facilities, but it has no authority, as it does in safeguards, to review states' physical protection measures.

60. U.S. Government Accountability Office, "Nuclear Nonproliferation IAEA Safeguards and Other Measures to Halt the Spread of Nuclear Weapons and Material," September 26, 2006, http://www.gao.gov/assets/120/114933.html.

believe that the nuclear export controls of the major nuclear suppliers are aimed at denying them nuclear technology and relegating them to a position of technical inferiority. These states have accused the nuclear suppliers of pursuing policies of political and commercial discrimination that are in conflict with, or go beyond, the requirements of the NPT. These concerns have been exacerbated by some proposals that have sought to ban the spread of enrichment and reprocessing technology. The United States and the other major nuclear suppliers have countered these charges by holding seminars to explain their controls; by publishing their regulations, laws, and agreements; and by making international guidelines fully transparent. The major nuclear suppliers should consider taking additional actions to consult with such states. While continuing to exercise special restraint in the transfer of sensitive nuclear technologies, the major suppliers should avoid taking initiatives that non-nuclear-weapon states regard as discriminatory, such as pressuring them to forswear nuclear capabilities that they regard as a sovereign right and one recognized in the NPT. Instead, they should offer positive incentives to forgo sensitive nuclear fuel-cycle technologies.

None of these steps by themselves will eliminate the proliferation risks of international civil nuclear commerce, but, taken together, they could go a long way toward strengthening the barriers to the misuse of civil nuclear commerce for nuclear explosive purposes.

4 THE ROLE OF THE UNITED STATES

The United States needs to take a leadership role in promoting the initiatives outlined above. It has many tools for furthering its nonproliferation objectives, not least of which is the political, military, and economic clout that it exercises in international affairs. One important instrument that it has employed for decades in building the nonproliferation regime has been its policy of attaching strict nonproliferation controls and conditions on its exports of nuclear fuel, reactors, technology, and fuel-cycle services. Washington has also been instrumental in establishing the international and multilateral nuclear trade controls described in this report. This was possible in no small part because of the technology and export dominance that the United States enjoyed from the 1950s through at least the 1970s.

However, even at the height of U.S. market dominance, nonproliferation controls were never easy to promote. Washington led the way in requiring consent rights, comprehensive safeguards, and dual-use controls and in restraining the transfer of sensitive nuclear technology. In some cases, it took a while for others to catch up to the United States. In other cases, the United States went too far, and its initiatives met with strong opposition from recipients as well as other suppliers. For example, the Carter administration's call for other advanced nuclear states to halt their reprocessing programs was roundly rejected. Similarly, the Bush administration's attempt to persuade the NSG to adopt a guideline barring the transfer of enrichment and reprocessing to countries that do not possess such technology met with stiff resistance from members of the NSG and strong criticism from non-nuclear-weapon states.

Over time, the number of suppliers has expanded while the U.S. role in the international nuclear market has declined significantly. In the 1950s and 1960s, the United States was the dominant supplier of nuclear materials, equipment, and technology, and it remained a major player for some years after that. Today, the United States is only one among many nuclear suppliers. Canada, China, France, Russia, South Korea, and others are already, or soon will be, major suppliers of nuclear fuel, reactors and related facilities, and fuel-cycle services.

A diminished U.S. role in the international nuclear market has important consequences. First, as other suppliers of nuclear materials and facilities have taken a larger share of the international nuclear market, the percentage of nuclear materials subject to U.S. nonproliferation controls has shrunk over time. Whether and to what extent the decline in the quantity of materials subject to U.S. controls, particularly consent rights, will weaken the effectiveness of the nonproliferation regime remain to be seen. However, it will clearly diminish U.S. influence with the fuel-cycle programs of importing states.

Second, most major nuclear suppliers do not have as rigorous or comprehensive national nuclear export conditions as those of the United States, and some members have given loose interpretations to NSG guidelines. The decline in the nuclear materials subject to U.S. agreements will mean that Washington has relinquished and will continue to relinquish its more stringent nonproliferation controls to those of other suppliers.

Third, the ability of the United States to exercise influence over the safeguards, physical protection, and other nonproliferation elements of other countries' civil nuclear programs will also decline. The United States may lose important person-to-person and laboratory-to-laboratory contacts with nuclear officials in other countries. Other suppliers will assume these valuable relationships. A decline in U.S. nonproliferation controls and influence is not in the interest of the United States, nor perhaps in the interest of the nonproliferation regime as a whole.

Fourth, the United States will find it increasingly difficult to impose onerous unilateral nonproliferation conditions on cooperating partners. Unilateral actions by themselves usually do not bring about desired results and can often be counterproductive. If potential importing states believe that the U.S. demands are excessive or that they deny them their rights, they can turn to alternative suppliers who can provide the nuclear materials, equipment, and technology they seek for their civil nuclear programs. It is, therefore, vital that the United States work closely with other suppliers in moving forward on the agenda outlined above, although reaching agreement may be painfully slow and not always to Washington's satisfaction. To continue to play a leadership role, the United States will need overcome the obstacles that are preventing it from competing effectively in the international market.

Some argue that one of these impediments is the stricter conditions that the United States imposes on its nuclear exports compared to other suppliers. This charge may contain a grain of truth. Some foreign utilities and their governments may think twice about purchasing U.S. nuclear equipment and enrichment services because of the extensive nature of U.S. consent rights and the conservative exercise of those controls by the United States in the past. After the Carter administration's grudging and protracted handling of reprocessing requests, some foreign utilities sought other sources of supply for enrichment services. Today, however, the United States is not challenging the fuel-cycle choices of other advanced nuclear states. Moreover, although members of the NSG do not implement the guidelines in a uniform manner, and some have loosely interpreted them, international nuclear trade rules among the major suppliers have been largely harmonized. Thus, the disparities in nuclear export controls between the United States and other suppliers have been greatly reduced. Whether the remaining existing disparities or new ones that may arise with new suppliers will affect U.S. competitiveness remains to be seen.

The U.S. nuclear industry has recently published a report concluding that the U.S. nuclear export control system is more complex, inefficient, and restrictive and places more onerous burdens on U.S. exporters than some of its key competitors in the international market.[61] The report concludes that the differences in the U.S. and non-U.S. export control regimes impose a competitive disadvantage on commercial nuclear exporters from the United States. While there is some validity to the report's argument that U.S. export laws and regulations may impose unnecessarily burdensome requirements on U.S. companies and that the approval of export applications may take an unreasonably long time, it is not clear that the U.S. system is causing serious damage to the competitiveness of the United States in the international market at the present time. Moreover,

---

61. James A. Glasgow, Elina Teplinsky, and Stephen L. Markus, *Nuclear Export Controls: A Comparative Analysis of National Regimes for the Control of Nuclear Materials, Components and Technology*, Nuclear Energy Institute, October 2012, www.nei.org/filefolder/ExportControlsComparativeAnalysis.pdf.

although the American regime for controlling nuclear exports should be streamlined and made more efficient, it is not the main reason for the decline in the U.S. share of the international market. Other factors are far more important:

- The emergence of other suppliers long ago undermined the monopoly of supply that the United States enjoyed in the early days nuclear energy. This was an inevitable development, and the future is likely to see the arrival of even more suppliers.
- The international playing field is not level. The nuclear export industries of other major suppliers have strong governmental and financial support that the U.S. nuclear export industry does not enjoy.
- The United States has not built new domestic nuclear power plants in over 30 years. Countries seeking to develop nuclear power are likely to turn for assistance to those states that have growing domestic nuclear power programs, offer competitive fuel-cycle services, and support the development of advanced technologies. Although U.S. skills in operating and regulating nuclear power plants are highly valued, manufacturing and construction effectiveness (which brings down costs) does not have the same credibility it once had. As a result, the ability of the United States to participate competitively in the international nuclear market has been weakened.

Overcoming these developments and obstacles will not be easy. Subsidies for U.S. nuclear exports may be one way to put American industry on a more competitive footing with nuclear exporters in other countries. However, financial support for U.S. nuclear exports has long been controversial and is likely to become even more so in the future, particularly in light of severe constraints on the U.S. budget.[62]

To retain a role in the international marketplace, some U.S. companies have entered into alliances with foreign suppliers. Toshiba's purchase of Westinghouse and the creation of General Electric1–Hitachi Nuclear Energy are examples of such ventures. However, it is not clear how the uncertain future of the post-Fukushima Japanese nuclear industry will affect these ventures. In any event, forging such alliances with foreign firms may be one avenue for promoting U.S. nuclear exports.

Revitalizing and rebuilding the domestic nuclear industry also faces significant challenges. The low price of natural gas plants and the absence of a national nuclear waste policy will significantly slow the nuclear renaissance, and post-Fukushima public concerns and new safety regulations may create additional brakes on nuclear power plant construction. However, the development of small modular reactors, if they prove economically competitive and meet safety standards, could not only rejuvenate the U.S. domestic nuclear industry but also boost the competiveness of the United States in the international market, particularly in developing countries. Although some have expressed concerns about the proliferation implications of laser isotope separation technology, if the General Electric-Hitachi Global Laser Enrichment Uranium Enrichment Facility, a venture

62. Some assistance may be feasible as the U.S. Export-Import Bank recently announced that it had authorized a $2 billion direct loan to Barakah One Co of the United Arab Emirates to purchase U.S. equipment and construction services to build a nuclear power plant in the UAE.

owned by GE, Hitachi, and Cameco Corporation, can satisfy proliferation concerns and meet the economic expectations of its supporters, it could give the United States a strong cost advantage in the global enrichment market. One step the United States could take to strengthen its role in the international market and promote its nonproliferation would be to establish a national nuclear waste program that would allow for taking back at least limited quantitites of spent fuel produced from U.S. nuclear exports. This may ultimately prove too hard to do, but it is well worth the effort.

Finally, the U.S. has to avoid overreach in instituting new nuclear export controls. Recent well-intentioned efforts by some in Congress and the Executive Branch to pressure other states to forswear enrichment and reprocessing capabilities could seriously damage the prospects for U.S. nuclear exports and deprive the United States of the nonproliferation influence that comes with nuclear cooperation.[63] Some have suggested other steps that would cause similar, if not more severe, damage to U.S. influence in international nuclear affairs.[64] Suppliers are not going to require such extreme export conditions, and most consumer states are likely to reject U.S. demands they believe deny them their rights or legitimate peaceful commercial opportunities.

The controls and influence that come with nuclear trade are only one tool in the U.S. arsenal to prevent the spread of nuclear weapons, but one that Washington can ill afford to let shrink further or wither away.

63. See Fred McGoldrick, "U.S.-UAE Peaceful Nuclear Cooperation Agreement: Gold Standard or Fool's Gold," Center for Strategic and International Studies, November 30, 2010, http://csis.org/publication/us-uae-peaceful-nuclear-cooperation-agreement-gold-standard-or-fools-gold.

64. For many examples of overreach, see Victor Gilinsky and Henry Sokolski, "Serious Rules for Nuclear Power without Proliferation," May 2012, http://carnegieendowment.org/2012/05/18/serious-rules-for-nuclear-power-without-proliferation.

APPENDIX
A NOTE ON PROPORTIONALITY AND CONTAMINATION AND U.S. CONSENT RIGHTS

The AEA does not contain any reference to either "contamination" or "proportionality." However, section 123 of the AEA establishes a requirement for various controls on nuclear material that is "used in or produced through the use of" nuclear material or equipment transferred under an agreement for cooperation. The question is what meaning to assign to this term as it appears in the AEA and in U.S. agreements for peaceful nuclear cooperation. "Used in" is straightforward. Any nuclear material used in a U.S. reactor becomes subject to all provisions of a U.S. agreement for peaceful nuclear cooperation. "Produced through the use of" is also straightforward up to a certain point:

- All plutonium generated in U.S.-obligated uranium is subject to all the provisions of an agreement, even if the production has taken place in a non-U.S. reactor.
- All plutonium generated in a U.S.-obligated reactor is subject all provisions of the agreement even if all the uranium fuel in which it is generated is non-U.S.-obligated.

A more complicated situation arises when plutonium is generated in a non-U.S.-supplied reactor in which part of the uranium fuel (or, in the case of a breeder reactor, the uranium blanket) is U.S.-obligated and part of it is not. In this situation, all the produced plutonium is subject to the safeguards, peaceful-use, and physical protection provisions of the U.S. agreement (the principle of "contamination"), but only some of the produced plutonium—the proportion produced in the U.S.-obligated fraction of the uranium—is subject to U.S. consent rights to reprocessing, retransfer, and so forth (the principle of proportionality). The same proportionality principle is used for assigning the consent-right obligations to the produced plutonium, for example, when the United States contributes some but not all of the nonnuclear material used in a non-U.S.-supplied reactor. In testimony before Congress on the first post-NNPA agreement with Australia, then assistant secretary of state Thomas Pickering explained that the principle of proportionality

> provides that our rights with respect to special nuclear material produced in a non-U.S.-supplied reactor will be exercised in proportion to the percentage relationship which the U.S. material used in the production of that special nuclear material bears to the total amount of material so used. It is important to understand, or underline that this proportionality applies only with respect to consent rights....It does not apply with respect to the central guarantees concerning no explosives or military applications and the safeguards, which cover fully all of the materials.[65]

65. U.S. Senate Committee on Foreign Relations, *The United States-Australian Agreement on the Peaceful Uses of Nuclear Energy: Hearing before the Committee on Foreign Relations*, 96th Cong., 1st sess., October 5, 1979, testimony of Thomas Pickering, Assistant Secretary, Bureau of Oceans and International Environmental and Scientific Affairs, Department of State.

To date, the United States had followed the strict principle of contamination in applying the peaceful-use guarantee to "produced" material. Whenever U.S. fuel is in a foreign reactor or whenever a U.S. reactor is being used, all the plutonium produced in that reactor may be used only for peaceful, nonexplosive purposes and must be subject to IAEA safeguards and adequate physical protection. The United States applies the principles of "contamination" and "proportionality" as described above to post-NNPA agreements for peaceful nuclear cooperation.

ABOUT THE AUTHOR

FRED MCGOLDRICK has extensive experience in nuclear nonproliferation and international nuclear policy fields. He held senior positions in the U.S. Department of Energy and the U.S. Department of State, where he negotiated U.S. peaceful nuclear cooperation agreements and helped shape U.S. policy to prevent the spread of nuclear weapons. He also served in the U.S. Mission to the International Atomic Energy Agency (IAEA) in Vienna. Since his retirement from the State Department, he has been a partner in Bengelsdorf, McGoldrick and Associates, LLC., an international consulting firm. He can be reached at ffmcg@comcast.net.